PETER GORDON KENDALL
1916 –1992

PETER GORDON KENDALL

Peter Gordon Kendall was born in Glasgow in 1916 and educated at Kelvinside Academy. After a year at the University of Glasgow he joined James Finlay & Co, and at the age of 22 was sent to India to join their Bombay office. At the outbreak of war, Peter enlisted in the Indian Army, obtaining an Emergency Commission. He was posted to Malaya in 1941 with the rank of Captain.

At the fall of Singapore in February 1942, Peter was taken prisoner together with all the surviving troops. Along with other Allied POWs he was interned in Changi Gaol, eventually moving from camp to camp through Malaya into Siam, working on the infamous Burma-Siam railway. His determination to survive the war kept him going through terrible hardship and distressing illnesses. On his release from captivity, he weighed only seven and-a-half stone.

Peter's post-war first marriage was dissolved in 1962. He subsequently re-married in his late forties and had two beloved sons of whom he was enormously proud. He died in 1992 after bouts of illnesses resulting from his time in captivity.

Peter's memoir *Surviving Changi* was written in 1982 and published in 2007 by his widow Sandra as part of the Kendall family archive.

Surviving Changi -
A MEMOIR

PETER
GORDON
KENDALL

SilverWood

Published in hardback by Silverwood Books 2007
www.silverwoodbooks.co.uk

Copyright © Peter Gordon Kendall & Sandra Kendall 2007

The right of Peter Gordon Kendall & Sandra Kendall to be identified
as the authors of this work has been asserted by them in accordance with
the Copyright, Designs and Patents Act 1988.

Illustrations published by courtesy of the Imperial War Museum, London
& The Sayle Literary Agency, Cambridge.
Copyright©Ronald Searle, 1939–1945.

ISBN 978-1-906236-01-4

British Library Cataloguing in Publication Data
A CIP catalogue record for this book is available from the British Library

To my wife Sandra

who was only two years old at the commencement of this story

and to my sons Nicholas and Anthony

who were born some twenty years after its conclusion

Peter Gordon Kendall
Hemingford Grey, Cambs
1982–83

CONTENTS

Changi Gaol 1942

FOREWORD

I must explain the discrepancy between the date this memoir was written and its eventual publication.

At the time my husband Peter began writing in 1982-83, he was waiting to be admitted to hospital for an operation. Recalling the war years and writing an accurate record of that time took his mind off the discomfort and the lengthy wait. I typed out the manuscript for him, but we never did anything further with it. The memoir was intended merely as a record for our family.

After Peter's death in 1992, I discovered the typescript and the handwritten manuscript in a drawer and made three or four Xeroxed copies for my sons and myself. However, these copies were not very satisfactory and I felt that neither my sons, nor my grandchildren when grown up, would be interested to read the material in that form.

It was only on re-reading the manuscript this year that I realised Peter's memories could be of interest to a wider public and decided they should be published in proper book form.

Surviving Changi is a fascinating record, both of a past era and of a horrendous prisoner-of-war experience, from which there is an ever dwindling number of survivors.

Sandra Kendall
Bristol
September 2007

INVICTUS

BY WILLIAM ERNEST HENLEY

Out of the night that covers me,
Black as the Pit from pole to pole,
I thank whatever gods may be
For my unconquerable soul.
In the fell clutch of circumstance
I have not winced nor cried aloud.

Under the bludgeonings of chance
My head is bloody, but unbowed.
Beyond this place of wrath and tears
Looms but the Horror of the shade,
And yet the menace of the years
Finds, and shall find, me unafraid.

It matters not how strait the gate,
How charged with punishments the scroll,
I am the master of my fate:
I am the captain of my soul.

MINUTE OF AGREEMENT between JAMES
FINLAY & CO.,LIMITED, Merchants,
22 West Nile Street, Glasgow, on
the First Part, and PETER GORDON
SHIRLEY KENDALL, 10 Victoria Circus,
Glasgow, W.2, on the Second Part.
The said Parties have agreed and do
hereby agree and bind and oblige
themselves as follows, viz:-

1.   The Second Party engages to enter the employment
of the First Party to serve as an assistant in their office
at Bombay or in such other capacity or in such other place
as may be directed by them from time to time, and he shall hold
himself in readiness to proceed to Bombay for that purpose when
requested by the First Party.

2.   The Second Party's engagement shall be for five years
from and after the date of his arrival at Bombay and entering
on his duties there but the First Party shall be entitled, in
their absolute discretion with or without reason assigned, at
any time during the currency of this Agreement to terminate
the engagement on giving three calendar months' previous notice
in writing to the Second Party of their intention so to do.
The First Party may, in lieu of notice, give the Second Party
by way of compensation a sum equivalent to three calendar months
of his salary, or, notice having been given, may at any time
dispense with the Second Party's services on paying him salary
for the unexpired portion of the time during which notice has
to run.   In the event of the agreement being determined by the
First Party under this clause, the First Party shall provide
the Second Party with a passage from Bombay to Great Britain
if he elects to proceed home at once, but not otherwise.

3.   The Second Party shall receive the following
remuneration for his services, viz:-

p.p. J.F. & Co.,Ltd.

14

During the 1st year at the rate of FIVE HUNDRED RUPEES (Rs.500) per calendar month.
During the 2nd year at the rate of FIVE HUNDRED AND FIFTY RUPEES (Rs.550) per calendar month.
During the 3rd year at the rate of SIX HUNDRED RUPEES (Rs.600) per calendar month.
During the 4th year at the rate of SIX HUNDRED AND FIFTY RUPEES (Rs.650) per calendar month.
During the 5th year at the rate of SEVEN HUNDRED RUPEES (Rs.700) per calendar month.

Further the Second Party's passage to Bombay shall be paid by the First Party.

4.   The Second Party shall, if required by the First Party, proceed to any part of India or Ceylon in connection with their business, they paying any extra expenses he may thereby incur, and shall remain there permanently or temporarily during the currency of this Agreement as may be required.

5.   The Second Party undertakes to devote his whole time and attention to the business and interests of the First Party, to discharge the duties of his situation diligently, faithfully and to the best of his ability, and not to communicate to third parties, or take with him at the close of his engagement, any patterns, copies of invoices, statistics, or other information connected with the business.

6.   The Second Party undertakes to conform to the rules of the business and in the event of his engaging in any unauthorised speculation or of his absenting himself from the duties of his situation on any occasion without the consent of the First Party (except in the case of unavoidable illness) or in the event of insubordination, neglect of duty, or breach of any of the provisions of this Agreement on his part, he shall be liable to dismissal without notice and shall forfeit his salary or such part thereof as may be due and unpaid at the time and all other rights under this Agreement.

7.   While the Second Party is at liberty to invest his savings in any legitimate manner, he engages not to enter into any share dealings or other transactions of a speculative

PG.3K

p.p. J.F. & Co.Ltd.

15

nature on his own account and not to connect himself in any way directly or indirectly with any undertaking outside of the business of the First Party without their written consent.

8. In the event of the return of the Second Party to Great Britain at the expiry of this engagement, but not in the case of its earlier termination from any cause, otherwise than is provided for in Clause 2 hereof (and provided he shall not have forfeited his rights in terms of Clause 6 hereof) he shall be entitled to a free passage to London or Liverpool as may be more convenient for the First Party.

9. Both Parties bind and oblige themselves to implement their respective parts of the premises to each other and in the event of failure on the part of either Party from any cause whatsoever, the Party failing shall be bound over and above performance to pay to the other Party in respect of each failure the sum of FIVE HUNDRED POUNDS sterling which is hereby fixed not as penalty but as liquidate damages.

10. The Second Party agrees to become a subscriber to the Home Provident Fund and to be bound by the Rules and Regulations of that Fund, a copy of which Rules and Regulations has been handed to him.

11. This Agreement shall be construed and receive effect according to the Law of Scotland and any questions, disputes or differences between the First Party and the Second Party or his representatives as to the true intent and meaning hereof or the carrying out of the same, including the ascertainment of sums due by either of the Parties to the other and all questions of liability for and assessment of damages shall, so often as they may arise, be referred to an Arbiter in Scotland to be appointed, failing agreement of Parties, by the Sheriff of Lanarkshire or any of his Substitutes at Glasgow on the application of either Party and the decision of such Arbiter, in arriving at

p.p. J.F. & Co.Ltd.

which he shall be entitled to take such expert or skilled
assistance as he may think necessary, shall be final and binding
on both Parties.

Signed per procuration by and on behalf of
    the said James Finlay & Co., Limited,
    Glasgow, by Alexander Muir McGrigor,
    Merchant, in presence of

per pro. James Finlay & Co.,Limited.

Signed by the said
    Peter Gordon Shirley
    Kendall in presence of

CHAPTER ONE

THE VOYAGE OUT
AUGUST 1938

When I set sail from Liverpool for India in the autumn of 1938, at the age of 22, little did I imagine that it would be over seven years before I saw England again. Nor did I imagine that the entire contents of the trunks accompanying me, which represented all my clothing and personal possessions, would be lost forever before I returned to England.

I had been working for the past four years in the Head Office of James Finlay & Co Ltd in Glasgow, and was being transferred to their Bombay offices. Under the terms of the first Agreement for overseas transfer, I was required to serve in India for an initial period of five years after which I would be granted six months home leave on full pay. Up to this time, the farthest I had strayed from the shores of Scotland was a short holiday in Jersey with my mother and occasional visits to England.

In retrospect, I now realise what a wrench my departure for five years abroad must have been for my mother and I remember the fortitude with which she bore it. She would now be on her own, having been divorced from my father for several years, but she did have her sisters and brother close at hand. However, wrapped up in the excitement of a new adventure, selfish youth seldom gives due weight to such matters, and my mother, of course, played it down.

I was seen off from Glasgow Central Station by a group of my friends who had previously wined and dined me at the Grosvenor Hotel. Mother came along, and I think enjoyed the outing. I know she was solicitously looked after by my friends after the train pulled out of the station. However, the prospect of new horizons and the excitement engendered by this tends to blunt the pangs of separation from loved ones and it is a truism that the sufferers in such a situation are those who are left behind.

I remember as though it were yesterday my arrival at Liverpool and my boarding of the SS *City of Hong Kong* bound for Marseilles, Port Said, Aden and Bombay. Liverpool, which I had never been to before, seemed a very lonely place on that afternoon in August 1938 as I knew nobody in the city and had to fend for myself for the first time. Fortunately, porters were available in abundance on railway stations at that time, and I managed to get my not inconsiderable luggage off the train and conveyed to the docks without mishap. My tin trunks and other baggage not wanted on voyage were labelled 'Hold' and were taken charge of by dockworkers and joined the stack of luggage on the quayside to be loaded in the hold.

Having organised the manhandling of my remaining luggage and seen it safely installed in my cabin, I wandered up on to the Promenade Deck. I remember standing at the rail of the ship watching anxiously as slings of baggage were lifted from the quayside and lowered into the hold, and praying that the rope sling wouldn't break and spew the contents of my beautiful, new tin trunks on to the wharf.

There were many passengers lining the rail, and I had an opportunity of studying those who were to be my travelling companions for the next three weeks – a motley crew, they seemed to be. Many were obviously seasoned travellers, having done this trip on more than one previous occasion. Some had families with them, usually either toddlers or daughters of marriageable age going out for the first time. At last, an announcement came over the tannoy for all visitors to go ashore and shortly afterwards the ship's hooter gave three short blasts and we cast off and slowly edged away from the dock.

The quayside was lined with people waving frantically to other people standing at the ship's rail. Everybody seemed to be waving and shouting farewells except me, so I decided to be less conspicuous and waved frantically to an imaginary figure standing amongst the crowd which was diminishing in perspective by the minute as the ship drew further and further away from the docks. As we steamed up the Mersey, the last of Liverpool one could see was the dome of the Royal Liver building outlined against the sky.

After unpacking and stowing my empty suitcases under the bunk, I found I had a reasonable amount of space in the cabin. I had enquired about dressing for dinner from a man who appeared to be a seasoned traveller, and had been informed that it was not customary to dress on first nights out of port or on last nights before docking. After a shower, I therefore donned a lounge suit and made my way to the bar half an hour before the dinner gong was due to be sounded. Everybody else, including ship's officers not on watch, did the same, and those people whom I had thought to be a motley crew of unfamiliar faces transformed themselves into individuals with an identity. Those of us on our own tended to gravitate together, and this process was assisted, to no mean extent, by the officers who mingled freely with the passengers and effected introductions.

There were no seating arrangements for dinner on this first night, so on the sound of the gong we descended, in groups, to the dining room and shared a table with those to whom we had been chatting in the bar. The food was out of this

SS City of Hong Kong

world, with a choice of seafood cocktail, melon or soup for starters, followed by fish, a choice of main courses, and finally a selection of sweets and biscuits with a plentiful cheese board. Wine was not included in the price of the ticket for the voyage, and it was the practice for those at each table to take it in turns to buy the wine for the meal.

All drinks ordered at the table or at the bar were purchased by signing a chit, and this was my introduction to the chit system, which operated throughout India and the East. No cash changes hands at the bars, and you are billed by being presented with a statement supported by a bundle of all the chits you have signed – at the end of each week on board ship, and at the end of the month in clubs. The largesse engendered by the bonhomie of shipboard life, combined with the fact that drinks are so much cheaper than ashore, causes many passengers to sign for large rounds of drinks at every opportunity and end up receiving relatively large bar bills at the end of the week. This can come as a considerable shock, and I remember one week receiving an envelope in my cabin that had split, being insufficiently large to house the huge bundle of chits I had somehow managed to sign during the previous seven days. It was on board the *City of Hong Kong* that I first learned the expression 'pencil shy' – the worst condemnation that can befall a man. On board ship, as elsewhere, you get all types, and just as there were some whose generosity was without bounds, there were others who always accepted, but never called, a round. After a time, they became known to everybody as 'pencil shy'.

After dinner it was necessary, if not vital, to take a bit of exercise and this was achieved on the dance floor. Coffee and liqueurs were served at the tables surrounding the small circle of parquet flooring allocated for dancing, and on this first night it seemed too large. An extremely good ship's band was doing its best and playing all the latest and most popular tunes of the time, but even the sound of Glenn Miller was not enough to prise the stuffed bodies of the audience off their seats. Eventually, it was the ship's officers who got the show on the road by getting up, crossing the dance floor and asking the lady of their choice to take the floor. That was all that was needed. Within a few minutes, the floor was packed with couples like sardines in a tin, and there was no need to know how to dance – there was no room to do anything but shuffle with the mob.

Next morning, before breakfast, I walked a brisk twenty times round the deck. No land was in sight, and a slight swell had developed – not enough, however, to put me off a full breakfast. This consisted of fruit juice or grapefruit, choice of cereal, kipper or smoked haddock with poached eggs, or eggs and bacon, tea, coffee or chocolate, toast and marmalade and newly baked rolls.

After breakfast, the slight swell had increased considerably as we had entered the Bay of Biscay which has the reputation of being rough, and this voyage was no exception. By noon the waves were mountainous and the ship rolled and pitched to an alarming degree. I remember sitting at the bar before lunch, perched on a high stool, when a gigantic wave caused all the glasses to be swept off the tables and the bar. The chairs and tables were anchored to the floor by chains, otherwise the damage would have been more severe.

Passengers who happened to be on their feet were thrown to the floor and slid to the side of the bar, ending up in a rather undignified position, but nobody was seriously hurt. The dining room was very empty that lunchtime and evening, but there was a lot of mess in companionways caused by passengers who hadn't quite made it to the nearest loo. Everyone was thankful when we passed through the Straits of Gibraltar, sailing quite close to the famous Rock, and entered the calmer waters of the Mediterranean. As the *City of Hong Kong* was a cargo-cum-passenger ship, the length of the voyage was increased by a call at Marseilles – at that time a real den of iniquity which seemed to be mainly populated around the dock area by sailors, dock workers and pimps. It was also an extremely unattractive and dirty city, or what we saw of it was.

We were allowed to go ashore in the evening and, accompanied by a chap of about my own age but whose name I forget, I visited various bars and ended up in a brothel – just for the experience. We must have got back on board sometime in the small hours as I was awakened by the sound of the breakfast gong lying fully clothed on my bunk. I could feel the throb of the ship's engine beneath me and see the flow of water through the porthole. We were well under way, and another day aboard ship was about to begin.

Obviously one can't recall events day by day as, apart from when we were in port, one day was much like another. A typical day would start with a walk round the Promenade Deck about twenty times before breakfast. Now that the weather had become warmer and the sea calmer, the sports facilities which the ship had to offer came into their own. After breakfast most passengers – other than the most lazy or infirm – would take to the sports deck, where there was a choice of deck tennis, deck quoits, shuffle board or table tennis. Then, of course, there was the open air swimming pool on a lower deck which was always filled with salt water, except in rough weather when it was emptied. Knockout competitions were organised for all the deck sports, plus darts, and entrants would enter their names on lists pinned up on the notice board. A draw was then made and a knockout table was compiled with byes, where necessary, and posted on the board. Rounds had to be played off by a fixed date, and the result entered by the winners. The eventual winner of each competition was presented with a prize at the Ball, which took place on the last night before arrival in Bombay.

There was also a bridge competition for the more sedentary, and the big gambling event was the daily estimate of the ship's mileage. About 11am each day, figures would be written in chalk on a blackboard at the stern end of the Promenade Deck. The central number would be the Captain's number, ie his estimate of the number of nautical miles travelled in the past 24 hours. Above and below this number would be the next ten higher and lower numbers, and at the end of the scale, top and bottom would be High Field and Low Field covering any number higher or lower than the twenty-one numbers on the board. Bets were one shilling each ticket and you could buy as many tickets covering as many numbers as you wanted, depending on how much you wished to invest. Each bet was recorded on the blackboard by a vertical line opposite the number. The actual mileage was conveyed from the bridge at noon, so the tote closed at 11.59am.

Most of the bets went on the Captain's number or the numbers up to five on either side of it. By going along at 11.55am, you could see which numbers had fewest bets on them and would therefore pay the highest odds. In this way it was sometimes possible to make a killing because the Captain could be quite far out in his estimate, whether deliberately or otherwise. I have won on High and Low fields on a number of occasions over the years.

I can remember little of the passengers. There was a family called Vecqueray – mother, father and daughter called Phoebe, who was one of the hearty types, and took no time in organising keep-fit classes on deck with daily meetings at 11am for press-ups, touch-toes, etc. She was a good-looking girl with a fine figure, but a bit too up-and-go for my liking. Some years later, she married a chap in Bombay called Lloyd – a rather quiet and placid type and quite popular in his bachelor days. Within a few years he literally ceased to exist as an individual, being known only as the husband of Phoebe Lloyd – she took him over and gobbled him up in the process.

The first smell of the East comes to one at Port Said, where we went ashore by walking across the pontoons which stretch from the quayside to the ship, as large vessels cannot come alongside because of shallow water close to the quay. Long before disembarkation, we were invaded by a score of bumboats selling everything you could buy ashore and at about twice the price. These traders had the advantage of tempting the first-time traveller before he knew the ropes, and many fell for it.

The bumboat man would first catch the eye of a prospective customer and would then throw up a rope with an accuracy perfected by experience. There

Health and Beauty class, with Phoebe second from right

could be as many as half a dozen ropes at a time thrown by different bumboat men to anyone standing at the deck rail who showed any interest in their wares. Then you were asked to shout down what particular item on display in the bumboat you would like to examine. It was duly put in a basket attached to the rope and hauled up by you for inspection. If you approved, you then started the ritual of haggling over the price, which is expected and allowed for, being part of the act.

Eventually, after some time, and usually after several rejections by you, if a price was finally agreed, you put the money in the basket, which is lowered down. After a really successful haggle, you could find you had only paid 25 percent more than the shop price – but then it was all good fun and much more entertaining than buying over the counter. At that time, shortly after the abdication of King Edward VIII, all women passengers were addressed as Mrs Simpson. The men, possibly because passengers up to then had been predominantly Scots, were all addressed as Mr McTavish.

The visit ashore was an experience in that you literally had to fight your way through a throng of youths, many not more than 8 or 10 years old, hanging on to your sleeve or any part of your attire they could grab hold of, and trying to sell you anything from dirty postcards to conducted tours of the red light area. A great coincidence was that they all had the same line of patter. "I take you to my sister, she very young and pretty – only sixteen." Having successfully fought off these hazards, you arrived at where you had set out for – Simon Arzt – the only multiple store in Port Said, which sold everything from leather camel stools to Persian rugs.

Most of the passengers on the *City of Hong Kong* had done the trip on many occasions, being either tea planters from up-country in India, or office staff from one of the cities who were known as *box-wallahs*. They were only too pleased to teach rookies like myself the ropes. It appeared that one of the 'musts' I had to buy was a *topee*, or pith helmet, from Simon Arzt. This piece of headgear was designed to protect the back of the neck, ostensibly to prevent one becoming a victim of sunstroke. Apart from the fact that it was extremely uncomfortable on the head, causing the top of same to sweat profusely, it also had the embarrassing tendency to take off with a sudden puff of wind, necessitating taking one's life in one's own hands by chasing after it as it rolled on its rim across a busy street with horns blaring from all directions. As likely as not, the *topee* had the sad fate of ending up squashed flat as a pancake before one could retrieve it. Presumably I became immune to the rigours of the tropical sun fairly rapidly, as I don't remember wearing my *topee* after the first few months in India.

The slow passage of the ship through the Suez Canal has become commonplace to me over the years, but that first experience of it in 1938 held an excitement I shall always remember. I recall standing at the bow of the ship watching the narrow strip of water ahead and the deserts of Egypt on one side and Sinai on the other slip slowly by, reluctant to tear myself away even for a meal. The passing point for vessels sailing in opposite directions was the Bitter Lakes, situated about half way through the canal. Here, the waterway widened out and a convoy of ships – passenger, cargo and oil tankers – would be waiting their turn to go through in the opposite direction.

There could be a bit of wait in the Bitter Lakes before the ship was allowed to enter the second half of the canal. Here the scenery was the same, with desert stretching as far as the eye could see on either side, broken by the odd oasis near the canal bank, with some buildings under a canopy of palm trees. Children would wave to us from these staging points as we steamed slowly past. The only other sign of life was the occasional Arab on a camel riding along the canal bank.

At Suez we entered the Red Sea, and from this point onwards the weather became extremely hot. The cabins, not being air-conditioned, were unbearable during the day, particularly on the starboard side which got the sun, and one avoided them except to sleep. Here I learnt that the word 'posh' was derived from the initials of 'port out, starboard home', referring to the more expensive side of the accommodation. Needless to say, being a *chokra*, or young lad, my cabin was on the wrong side – the starboard side. I wasn't posh!

Memories of the Red Sea conjure up a glass-like surface with flights of flying fish skimming across the surface for fifty yards or so before plunging back into the water. Also, schools of porpoises cartwheeling ahead of the ship, disturbed by the movement of the water.

The next port of call was Aden – the rock projecting starkly out of the sea and devoid of vegetation, as aptly described in the famous Scottish Pipe Band tune *The Barren Rocks of Aden*. Aden was a refuelling port and we were allowed to go ashore. There was not a lot to see, but if you could summon up the energy in the intense heat to walk up the path that led to the summit of the rock, you were rewarded by the sight of the Barbary apes which abounded there. These apes were so tame they would take a banana from your hand, and they were the main tourist attraction on the island. The other attraction was the caves on the east side of the rock, which I visited on a later occasion.

The last lap of the voyage was from Aden through the Arabian Sea, and the night before arrival at Bombay there was a Gala fancy dress dance, when prizes were presented for all the sports competitions which had helped to offset the effect of the fabulous eating on our waistlines. There were also prizes for the best male and female fancy dress costume.

Although this turned out to be a late night, I was up at 6am to get my first glimpse of Bombay as it appeared through a heat haze.

The early morning sunshine shimmered on the golden basalt stone of the Gateway of India, highlighting the four turreted towers and the imposing central dome. Boats dotted the harbour and I could just make out a multitude of tiny figures swarming up and down the steps to the waterfront.

After the long weeks at sea, I had finally arrived in Bombay!

Port Said, 1938
with new topee!

28

CHAPTER TWO

THE OUTRAM HOTEL, BOMBAY
SEPTEMBER 1938 – JANUARY 1939

On arrival in Bombay docks, a representative from our office met me, and helped me to identify and collect my various trunks after they had been off-loaded from the hold. He then conveyed my luggage and me to the Outram Hotel, which was within a short distance of our office.

The Outram Hotel was not one of the most salubrious hotels of Bombay – in fact it was at the opposite end of the spectrum from the Taj Mahal Hotel which, however, was located close by. The Outram was situated on the third floor of a building, the first two floors of which were let out as offices. During my short stay the lift was permanently out of order, so on reaching one's room after the effort of climbing three flights of stairs to reach it, one required at least five minutes sitting under the *punkah*, or overhead fan, to dry off.

This being the month of October, the heat and humidity in Bombay were at their most severe, and the sweat literally drained from the pores at all times of the day and night unless you were in an air-conditioned room. The Outram Hotel did not rise to air-conditioning. The bed was provided with an overhead framework supporting a mosquito net, which was rolled up during the day. On my first night I realised the importance of that net as, around dusk, I started to hear the high-pitched whine of countless mosquitoes and feel their effect on any bits of exposed flesh. Even the ankles and calves, although covered, were not immune, as access could be obtained up the trouser legs.

One's room was not a healthy place to sit around in after dusk, and it was my practice to stay out until time for bed and then get under the net as quickly as possible. The net, while keeping out the mosquitoes, unfortunately kept out a lot of the breeze from the *punkah*, so one lay on top of the sheets in pyjama bottoms only, while the sweat trickled in rivulets down one's chest. The hotel was deemed by the powers that be in James Finlay & Co Ltd to be a suitable abode for a young assistant on his first contract and on a starting salary of 500 rupees per month – about £40 at that time.

There are many things other than the degree of humidity prior to, during, and just after the monsoon that come as a surprise – if not a shock – to the new arrival in Bombay. One tended to get used to these and treat them as commonplace over the years. The smell of the East, which I mentioned at Port Said, hits you the moment the ship ties up in Alexandra Dock and becomes more pungent as one is driven from the docks, through the bazaars, towards the business and residential areas of the city. On that drive, one also registers with shock the extent of the poverty that exists: the beggars sitting on the pavements, the children following your car as it travels through the crowded streets, all of them begging for alms every time it is brought to a halt by the mass of humanity spilling on to the road. Many of these beggars and children had physical defects, such as a stump for an arm or leg, a nose eaten away by leprosy, or arms and legs like spindles and the whole rib cage visible through emaciation.

Another sight one got used to over the years, were the emaciated cows, which roam freely through the streets and bazaars with no apparent owner. The cow is sacred in India, and Hindus cannot eat beef from the cow for religious reasons. Beef in India is invariably buffalo meat and cows are allowed to live on till eventually they drop down from old age or starvation or malnutrition. One should also not be surprised to meet the odd *sadhu*, or religious man, walking along the road stark naked, his body and face grey from ashes that have been rubbed on.

A visit to the stalls in the bazaars and market also brings its surprises. Flies in their thousands settle on anything tasty, such as a wedge of water-melon, or a cut of meat. And everywhere – but everywhere – you have children or beggars pulling at your sleeve or doing a *salaam* in front of you from their squatting posture on the pavement, and rattling a tin can containing a few *pice*, which was at that time the smallest unit of currency. The coins were those that he or she has been lucky enough to obtain from those more fortunate in life.

Many of the beggars are cripples from birth, but it does happen that bones of small babies are deliberately broken or malformed shortly after birth to increase their earning capacity as beggars in a land where there is no work for the scheduled castes. These are the Untouchables – the lowest of the many castes, headed by the Brahmins, which make up the vast population of the sub-continent of India. It is surprising to the visitor to India how strongly the caste system operates after over a century of British rule. Perhaps it is endemic to India, in that after forty years of independence the caste system still prevails, and it is difficult for the foreigner to reconcile a socialist society with such a system.

On reporting to the office on the Monday morning, I was given a briefing on my duties and a long pep talk by Andrew Geddes, the *Burrah Sahib* or Managing Director. He told me I would be assigned to the Mills department and would spend my first six months at our three textile mills in different suburbs of Bombay, under training from the mill superintendent. This would entail going to a mill from my hotel – a distance of about eight miles – for which a car and driver would be provided. I would lunch with the superintendent at his bungalow on the Finlay Mill premises and, after further instruction in the afternoon, be dropped back at my hotel around 6pm.

During these six months, I would be instructed in the technique of cotton identification and the processes of spinning, weaving, bleaching, cloth and yarn dyeing and, finally, finishing. I would also do a course at Swan Mill where, in addition to spinning and weaving, we had a plant for the manufacture of tyre cord under contract to The Firestone Tyre & Rubber Co. The importance of keeping fit and loyalty to the Company which was employing me at this princely salary, was also stressed.

"Keep your bowels open and your mouth shut!" said Mr Geddes.

I learnt that I was expected to join the Gymkhana Club – the Gym for short – which provided most sports including rugby, tennis and squash. It also had two billiard tables. It was very much the young man's club, and the entrance fee and monthly subscription were modest, unlike other clubs such as The Royal Bombay Yacht Club and the Willingdon Sports Club which were well beyond the means of an assistant on his first contract.

The Gym was ideally situated, with parkland called the Maidan occupying the entire frontage and stretching away for about half a mile from the grassy lawns of the Club. Along the front of the building was a covered veranda where one sat of an evening after a game enjoying a small measure of whisky, known as a *chota peg*, in the cool air from the overhead *punkahs* revolving slowly. On dance nights, except in the monsoon season, tables were moved out from the veranda on to the lawn, and on one night a week the Police Band played light music on the lawn between 7pm and 9pm.

The Club employed a large number of bearers, the senior of whom were called butlers, who looked smart in the Club uniform of turbans, white trousers and 'bum freezer' jackets, with green waistcoats for the bearers and red waistcoats for the butlers. One soon got to know all the bearers by name, as they got to know yours.

The method of ordering a round of drinks, cigarettes or snacks was simple. You caught the attention of the bearer by raising your hand. All the bearers and butlers carried chit books, and he would write your order on the top chit which you would sign. This chit was presented to the barman who would place your order on a tray that the bearer brought back to your table. At the end of the month, the amount of the monthly subscription was usually an insignificant percentage of the total bill, and I remember never being able to believe that I had signed so many chits. You could usually hazard a guess at the size of the bill by the thickness

31

of the envelope contents – the thicker the package, the more chits it contained. A feature of the chits accompanying the Club bills, was the increasing illegibility of the signature as an evening progressed, and you could almost pinpoint the time a chit had been signed depending on the degree of illegibility.

The Gym was very much a social club where one met the young debutantes – for lack of a better name – brought out from England for the cold weather, from November to April, to visit their parents. They were known locally as 'the fishing fleet'. It was the earnest hope of parents of daughters of marriageable age, and of the daughters themselves, that they would find themselves a potential future husband in the six months available to them before being sent back to the arid shores of England. The Gym held twice weekly dances at which the girls had the opportunity of meeting the local stags that far outnumbered them. Unfortunately for the debs, the large majority of the stags preferred to prop up the bar, playing liar dice or just chatting in the earlier part of the evening. As the bar was out of bounds to the female sex, dances tended to have a preponderance of females in attendance during the first couple of hours, who sat hopefully around the circumference of the dance floor. In the last hour there was invariably an invasion of well oiled gentry to the floor to sweep the girls off their feet – literally!

There were no immediate prospects for 'the fishing fleet' as far as James Finlay & Co and many other similar companies were concerned, because it was written into our contracts that marriage would not be permitted until our third agreement. As the first two agreements were for five and four years respectively, this speaks for itself.

Life living in the Outram Hotel during my first few months in Bombay was not exactly idyllic, and I consequently spent very little time there except to sleep, apart from an hour each evening when I was expected to get down to learning Urdu, the official *lingua franca* of India. I should mention here that English was widely spoken and understood in the cities. It was spoken fluently by all the clerical staff in the offices, as well as by most of the servants, who spoke a form of pidgin English, and all the bearers employed by the large European community. However, a knowledge of Urdu was essential if one travelled up-country, though in certain States, particularly in South India, Urdu was of little use as local languages such as Maharati, Gujerati or Konkani were spoken. There are several hundred of these local languages and dialects spoken in the many regions that comprise India.

The aim of all office assistants arriving in India for the first time, was to pass the Lower Standard Urdu Exam and eventually the Higher Standard, both set by the local Chamber of Commerce. With this end in view, all assistants were obliged to employ a *munshi*, or teacher, who came to one's residence thrice weekly for an hour at the going rate of 30 rupees per month. My *munshi* used to roll up at the Outram Hotel, where he would squat on the floor of my room, cross-legged, and try to instil the basic rudiments of the language into my brain, which by this time in the evening, after a long day, was not at its most receptive. The frequent distractions of swiping at mosquitoes, or scratching bites, didn't help the concentration.

My *munshi* continued his thrice weekly visits to me after I moved thirteen miles out of the city to Santa Cruz, though I never did find out how he got there and back. The reward – or bribe, if you like – from the firm for passing the Lower Grade exam was 200 rupees, and for passing the Higher Grade exam, 500 rupees – a princely sum, representing a whole month's salary. I achieved the former, but never the latter, as the war intervened.

On weekdays the car picked me up at 7.30am and took me to one of the mills, where I spent the day. The humidity inside the mill was boosted by overhead humidifiers that sprayed the steam imperative to the process of spinning and weaving of cotton textiles. The hour off for lunch at the Superintendent's bungalow was a welcome break, during which I could ask questions about some of the technicalities. I got back to the hotel around 6pm, and after a very necessary shower and change of clothing, I used to walk round to the Gym for either a rugger practice on Tuesdays and Thursdays, or a game of squash or tennis. This was followed by another shower and change of clothes in the very spacious men's changing room. Then on to the Bar, which occupied two walls of a huge room, where we could unwind and either chat or play liar dice for tins of cigarettes – round tins of fifty cigarettes costing 1 rupee and 8 annas, which was about 13 pence.

At weekends I used to go off either to Breach Candy or Juhu. The former is an immense open-air, salt water swimming pool of irregular shape, situated next to the sea, with snack bar, lawns with coloured umbrellas, and an ambience of luxury. It is situated below Cumballa Hill, a smart residential area about three miles from the business centre. Juhu is a beach of silver sands bordered by shacks and beach houses engulfed in coconut palms. The beach stretches for about four miles and is situated about sixteen miles from Bombay.

Roberts, Farr and friend at Juhu Beach, 1939

Breach Candy swimming pool, 1939

Juhu Beach

CHAPTER THREE

SANTA CRUZ
JANUARY – MAY 1939

After I had been in Bombay for a short while, a friend suggested that I should move away from the Outram Hotel and go to live at the Light Horse Camp at Santa Cruz. This would necessitate my joining the Bombay Light Horse, which was a Territorial Unit of the Reserve Forces of India, and, as I had never ridden a horse, undergoing instruction in that art. This, however, was a small price to pay to get away from the claustrophobic room at the Outram Hotel. Having joined, I would be permitted to live at the camp until it closed down early in June at the start of the monsoons.

Early in January 1939, I therefore transferred myself, bag and baggage, to Santa Cruz – about 15 miles from Bombay, near the airport – and had the advantage of being on the spot for early morning riding instruction.

Life for me at the camp took on a new dimension as I enjoyed living virtually in the country and quickly made a number of very good friends who influenced my life in the immediate future to a large extent. We used to wake in the morning at 6am to the sound of horses' hooves pawing the ground outside our huts. After pulling on jodhpurs and riding boots, and slipping a khaki shirt over the head (no time for a wash or shower), we would be in the saddle by 6.10 and riding to the parade ground accompanied by the *syce* on his horse. We were then drilled for an hour by the Sergeant Major – a chap called Giddings – in persuading the horse to do a right turn, a left turn, an about turn, and to walk, canter or gallop when you wanted it to perform these feats, and not when the horse wanted to. We also had sessions in the jumping ring where you were expected, along with the horse of course, to clear a series of small hurdles, each about one foot high. I say along with the horse, because some of us found it much easier to clear the hurdle without the horse, which remained with its front legs planted firmly in the ground on the other side.

After about a week of rigorous instruction from Sergeant Major Giddings, who was a British Cavalry Warrant Officer, we were allowed to leave the parade ground and venture across the vast expanse of open country which was Santa Cruz at that time. I shall never forget my first jaunt out of the riding ring. I set out across the beautiful open country to which I referred. The terrain was flat but interspersed with *bunds*, or dykes, that separated the various fields or parcels of land. Everything went extremely well on the way out, with the horse responding to the signals by changing the pace and by jumping the fairly low *bunds*.

I began to think this was a bit of a doddle, and after going for about a mile decided to head for home. That was when the trouble started. My horse decided that he wanted to get back for his feed of oats in the shortest possible time by the most direct route, and no amount of pulling on the reins had any effect on this resolve. We literally flew through the air at a gallop, with me clinging on to the horse's neck for dear life. We might have made it without mishap had there not been a tree with a low horizontal branch in our direct path. As we approached at a thundering pace, there was no way I could divert the horse's course and there was no way I could get myself under the branch. The result was that I ended up prostrate on the ground while the horse became an ever smaller dot on the landscape as he headed in the most direct route for his oats. I remember picking myself up painfully and trudging slowly back to camp, knowing the riderless horse would be already there and that everybody would know whose it was. I suffered a lot of lost pride and ragging when I got back.

Before moving out to Santa Cruz I had invested in a second-hand T Type MG sports car. I remember it was red, but don't remember how I paid for it. I know it can't have been out of my salary of 500 rupees a month, so I must have presumably taken some savings out from England with me. Anyhow, I found the MG very useful to get me from the camp to the Mills and back in the evening. In this respect it was a godsend as there was no way I could have got the use of an office car for this trip.

In March I finished my training at the Mills and from then onwards spent my working day in the office in town. On weekday mornings the red MG, with hood down in order to create as much air as possible, would be seen traversing the coast road between Santa Cruz and Bombay around 8 or 8.30am I would be accompanied by one of my friends, usually Brian Woodley – Woody to his more intimate group – who didn't have a car. We would be dressed in the standard uniform for young office assistants, or *chokras,* of white drill trousers, white cotton long-sleeved shirt, tie, and beige cotton unlined jacket. The latter item lay folded on the back seat of the car and was only donned on arrival at the office. This was not as a sign of respect, but to allow one's shirt to dry off slowly in the air-conditioning without giving one pneumonia in the process. After the shirt had dried in half an hour or so, the jacket was hung on a hanger in one's room behind the desk where it remained until the evening.

When I first arrived in Bombay, the company provided me with a bearer, or personal servant, who looked after my clothes, served meals, including *chay* and *chottha hazri* (tea and early morning breakfast), made the bed and generally kept my quarters clean and tidy. One came to rely on one's bearer for everything (and I'm told I still do, though he hasn't been around for nigh on 20 years!).

In travelling up-country in India, or in my case on the move to Santa Cruz, your bearer always accompanied you. He slept outside your room on a *dhari* or cloth mat and was responsible for getting you up in time in the morning – not always the easiest of tasks. John (the Joogler) Milligan, a very sound sleeper, was renowned for bawling out his bearer for failing to get him up in time. His bearer's protestations that he had been trying to rouse *Sahib* for at least twenty minutes but that on each occasion he approached him, *Sahib* got very angry and shouted "B...... off" – fell on deaf ears.

There was an obvious advantage in keeping the same bearer as long as possible. For one thing, he got used to your ways and idiosyncrasies, and for another a kind of loyalty built up over the years between the bearer and his *sahib* and this loyalty – call it even affection – was not entirely one-sided.

On return from a day's work, it was the custom – and very necessary – to have a shower and don fresh clothes for the evening similar to those worn during the day, unless going to a dinner party when DJs were normally worn. The washerman, known as a *dhobi*, was kept busy: two pairs of trousers, two shirts, two vests and two pairs of socks came to him for washing from each *sahib* each day. He was paid on a monthly basis, at that time 35 rupees a month (about £2).

The method of washing was to convey all the clothes to the *dhobi ghat* – usually the bank of a rather muddy river on which flat rocks abounded. The clothes were then immersed in the water, soaped and beaten with force against the flat rocks that knocked the dirt, not to mention most of the stuffing, out of them. They were then ironed and liberally starched to put back some of the stuffing removed by the beating to which they had been subjected, and delivered back to the bearer.

More often than not, due to the harsh treatment, buttons were broken, and the bearer would spend some time each day to sew on buttons or repair other damage. How the *dhobi* knew which clothes belonged to which household, I never found out, but I suspect the bearers assisted in identifying their own sahib's clothes, sheets, towels, etc.

My bearer
taken outside Light Horse Camp, Santa Cruz, 1939

CHAPTER FOUR

BOMBAY – CHUMMERY LIFE
JANUARY 1939 – JANUARY 1940

As the Light Horse camp only remained open for six months of the year, everyone staying there had to look for alternative accommodation at the end of that period. Life amongst young expatriates centred around the chummery. The chummery can be described as a group of three or more males who, for reasons of friendship and companionship, not to mention economy, decide to share either a flat or a bungalow and the expenses connected with the running thereof. The accommodation became available when families returned home to England on furlough, and as furloughs were never for periods longer than six months, chummeries were constantly on the move from one abode to another, never being static for longer than six months.

As the date for closure of the camp approached, a group of my closest friends and I decided to form a chummery. They were Woody, Bruce Gilbertson (Gilby) fromWanganui, New Zealand, Drummond Black (Blackie), John Milligan, Peter Scarlett and myself. It happened that the closure of the camp coincided with the departure on six months leave of the Chief Justice of Bombay, Chief Justice and Lady Blackwell. Somehow we got word of this and, as it was ideal for our requirements.

We entered into an arrangement known as a *bandhobast*, whereby the six of us would take over their very opulent bungalow and extensive garden which was situated on Cumballa Hill, a very fashionable residential area of Bombay about four miles from the business centre of the city.

The bungalow had two floors, the ground floor consisting of the reception rooms and a large veranda along the front overlooking a garden of bougainvillaea and other colourful shrubs bordering a superbly kept lawn. The entrance drive culminated at the front steps leading up to the veranda. The upper floor had five bedrooms and a private suite consisting of bedroom, bathroom and its own small veranda. The privilege of occupying the suite was decided one evening by a game of liar dice at the Gymkhana played over several beers and won by John Milligan.

The Blackwells charged us a very modest rent, as most families preferred to have their accommodation occupied rather than lying empty during their absence. The humidity and heat play havoc on the walls, woodwork and furniture over a long period, and deterioration due to the formation of mould can be a costly business. Occupation ensures the running of the air-conditioners in the bedrooms

Our chummery, June 1939 to January 1940
back left to right: John Mulligan, Lon Williams
middle: Bobby Longwill, Brian "Woody" Woodley
bottom: Blackie, Rusty the dog, Chris Miller

and the movement of the *punkahs* in the reception rooms at regular intervals thereby preventing the formation of mould. The damage can be far more severe in the high humidity of the monsoon when most expatriates tended to go on leave, and during that period some felt it almost preferable to let their flat or bungalow free rather than have it lying empty for six months.

During the six months we occupied the Blackwells' bungalow, the six of us lived in the lap of luxury and well above the standard enjoyed by the average *chokra* on his first agreement. The establishment consisted of our six personal bearers. A butler was left and maintained by the Chief Justice, to keep an eye on their possessions and ensure that the ornaments, furniture, etc. were dusted regularly by our bearers, and that the minimum of damage was caused by the six rather high spirited occupants during their absence. The butler was also entrusted with maintaining a list of glass and crockery breakages. There were two gardeners, called *malis*, maintained by the Blackwells to look after the garden, and we employed a cook and a *hamal* or sweeper.

The arranging of menus and the handling of the Cook's 'book' was entrusted to Woody. A word here about the system of the Cook's 'book' in India might be of interest. This book, usually a small notebook, was maintained on the imprest system. At the start, the Cook would be put in funds by an advance of twenty or thirty rupees, and this figure was reduced daily as the Cook entered the cost of his purchases, item by item, and subtracted them. When the balance approached zero, it was topped up by a further round sum advance.

Every evening the Cook would produce a suggested menu for the following day for approval, and also the book that had been written up with the current day's bazaar purchases. It was a recognised fact that all cooks made a bit on the Cook's 'book' and this was accepted. Unless there was an outrageous discrepancy in a price charged for a particular item or a substantial error in addition or subtraction, prices for daily purchases of meat, vegetables, fruit, eggs etc, and other culinary necessities, were not usually queried. Lunches were only required at weekends and then often for only some of us, as there was quite a lot of dining out. Most offices were equipped with 'tiffin' rooms where free lunches were supplied to the executive staff five days a week.

The period we lived in the Blackwell bungalow passed all too quickly, and early in November 1939, I teamed up with Gilby, Woody and Blackie to form a chummery in the ground floor flat of Gold Cornet, near the bottom of Gamadia Road, also on Cumballa Hill and not far from Breach Candy swimming pool.

An interesting postscript to the Blackwell episode happened around mid-November when a committee of two was summoned by Lady Blackwell to discuss

Our mali (gardener)

John Mulligan in his Morris

Bombay 1939
Just out of bed with a bad hangover!

a financial settlement by us for certain breakages that had occurred during our period of residence. Blackie and I represented the chummery at the meeting, when the butler produced a list of broken items of glass and crockery, which we did not dispute and agreed to settle. The amount involved was small, as we had only been left very ordinary glass and crockery, the crystal and Spode having been carefully locked away during our tenancy.

We were about to take our leave, when Lady Blackwell drew our attention to a bronze head that stood on a pedestal next to the door leading from the drawing room to the veranda. This rather valuable object had certain indentations on its surface which Lady B assured us had not been there when she and her husband went on leave. Being quite unprepared for this query, I hastily improvised a reply to the effect that it may have been accidentally knocked over on some occasion. Imagine our consternation when Lady B, drawing herself up to her full height, announced, "This is not what happened according to my butler. He tells me that on the occasion of Mr Woodley's birthday, it was rolled down the front steps into the garden!"

By the time we moved to Gold Cornet, war had broken out in Europe and the Bombay Light Horse, along with the other auxiliary unit, the Bombay Motor Patrol, were mobilised and combined to form the Bombay Light Patrol (B.L.P.) Horses were replaced by motor cycles. On mobilisation, offices were obliged to release those members of their staff involved at certain times on specific days of the week for exercises in security. These, I seem to remember, involved dashing around Bombay on a motor cycle, conveying top secret messages from one headquarters to another. I remember many such trips ending up at the Army barracks at the far end of Colaba Causeway, having started from a house in Malabar Hill, a distance of some four miles or so. At that time, motor cycles tearing hell for leather long the sea front of Marine Drive in both directions were a common sight.

I had now been working at Finlay & Co's offices at Flora Fountain for six months, having completed my technical training period at the three Mills for which we acted as Managing Agents. This system is peculiar to the East where the Managing Agents act in the capacity of Manager of the managed company instead of an individual Manager. In the case of the Mill companies, each was a public limited company in which James Finlay & Co held at that time a majority shareholding. The Manager of James Finlay & Co, Bombay, was always automatically Chairman, and two other senior executives were on the Board of Directors of the three Mill companies. However, at the time of which I write, I was far from the dizzy heights of the Boards, having just completed the first year of my first agreement.

CHAPTER FIVE

BELGAUM
FEBRUARY – MAY 1940

In October 1939, an Officers' Training School (OTS) was inaugurated in Belgaum and many of the British community from all over India attended the various courses lasting four months, which ran consecutively from that time. Having obtained permission from my *Burrah Sahib*, I set off for Belgaum at the end of January 1940 to join the second course, where I was posted to B Company under the command of Major Tucker.

The course involved ground exercises called TEWTS (Tactical Exercises Without Troops), Leadership, Map Reading, and allied subjects. At the end of the four months, unless you were a complete nitwit, you were expected to pass out with an Emergency Commission as a 2nd Lieutenant. This was some difference from the length of the course at Sandhurst for obtaining a commission in the regular army in peacetime. However, it was essential to expand the size of the Armed Forces in India in the shortest possible time, including their officer content.

The particular course I attended had no fewer than seventeen members of James Finlay & Co staff, from their various offices and tea estates throughout India. There were four from the Bombay office, John Burns, Colin Campbell, Bobby Longwill and myself. Two others, 'Coffee' Roy and Lindsay Muir, tea planters from our South India tea estates, had been in the head office in Glasgow while I was there. I had attended the farewell party given for them on an evening in 1937 when, after wining and dining, they were seen off from Glasgow Central Station by their many friends. Also on the course was Ian Murison who was later to become Manager of our Calcutta office.

I had taken the MG to Belgaum and found it very useful for getting away at weekends when we were off duty and seeing a bit of South India. I also used it to go with a friend for mid-term leave at the end of March. That was a memorable trip. We drove overnight to Bombay hitting a bullock amidships en route, which inflicted a serious dent in the radiator, but seemed to do little damage to the bullock, which picked itself up with alacrity and took off into the undergrowth. The road from Belgaum to Bombay was little used by traffic at night. It had thick undergrowth and woods on either side and was unfenced. As we found out to our cost, it was quite common for wildlife or sheep or bullocks to wander across the road, and in the dark there was little or no warning of their presence. I seem to remember that the cooling system was still intact and that after disengaging the mud-guard from the front wheel, we were able to proceed to Bombay and booked in at the Taj Mahal Hotel the following morning.

We spent four glorious days in Bombay, mainly lying in the sun and swimming at Breach Candy, before driving back to Belgaum for the second half of the course.

The mid-term break was very necessary as the training schedule was rigorous, to say the least. Four Companies, A, B, C and D, each commanded by a Major or Lieutenant Colonel, with British regular army Sergeant Majors in charge of platoons, made up the establishment. The Sergeant Majors had the unenviable task of converting *box-wallahs* used to working in business or commerce, and tea planters with little or no military training, into Officers in the ridiculously short period of four months.

To accomplish this, every available hour of the day had to be utilised. *Reveille* was sounded at 6.30am and we had to be on the parade ground, properly dressed for inspection, at 7am. Dress was khaki shorts and shirt, khaki stockings and puttees, and boots polished so you could see your face in them.

After inspection, we went off in groups to various areas in the open country surrounding Belgaum, where mock attacks on predetermined targets were planned and executed. This involved best utilisation of natural cover between your position and the target to be captured. We returned to camp around 9am for breakfast, after which we had lectures and exercises in map reading and strategy. In the afternoon there were more TEWTs and lectures finishing about 6pm with a parade prior to being dismissed.

We were expected to parade smartly at all times and obey commands with precision. I remember on one particular evening, when we had had an extremely exhausting day under an over-zealous Sergeant Major. The Warrant Officers always addressed the trainees as "Mr So-and-so Sir", and the following episode caused much laughter in the ranks when it took place. One of our number was a fellow called Popple (who was later awarded an MC and Bar) who on the command "Cover off" – being tired and not registering properly – did a right turn as is normal prior to dismissal.

Quick as a flash came a bawl from the Sergeant Major, "Mr Popple Sir, I said cover off, not bugger off!"

Towards the end of the course, we were required to list three Regiments, in order of preference, to which we would like to be posted on being commissioned. I chose the 17th Dogra Regiment, the 1st Gurkha Regiment and the 2nd Gurkha

Regiment in that order. The only reason I had for choosing these Regiments was that they were composed of only one religious caste, and consequently much easier to administer. By comparison, the Punjab, Sikh, Gharwal and Jhat Regiments were composed of four Companies, each of which could be of a different caste.

I was glad, when I read the list posted on the notice board, to find that I had got my first choice, and even more so to see that I would be posted to the 2nd Battalion which was stationed in Malaya.

I must confess that I had no great burning desire to rush post haste to confront the enemy with my vast experience of four months learning how to be a soldier.

This seemed to me to be the luck of the draw or the will of God. Had I been posted to the 1st Battalion of the Dogra Regiment, I would have been operating in the Western Desert, where my good friend John Milligan was wounded, taken prisoner and subsequently died of his injuries.

Belgaum, May 1940
back left to right: 2nd Drummond Black "Blackie", 3rd Bobby Longwill, 4th myself
middle: 2nd Brian "Wood" Woodley, end Colin Campbell (Bombay office)
front: centre Sir John Burns (MD James Finlay & Co, Bombay),
end right Ian Muirison (Calcutta office)

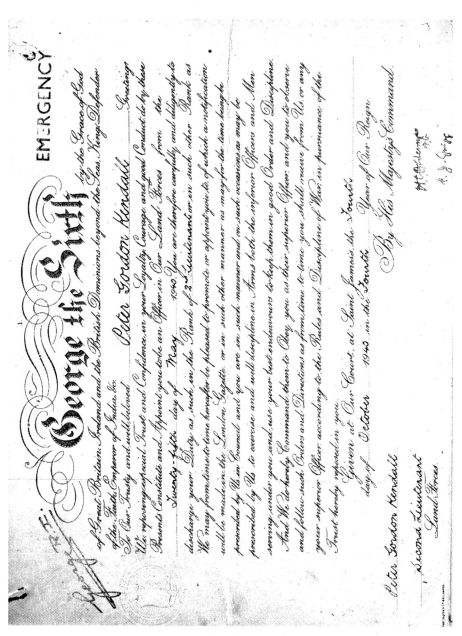

Emergency Commission

CHAPTER SIX

JULLUNDER
JUNE – OCTOBER 1940

At the end of the fourth month after going to Belgaum, I attended a passing out parade and was issued with a single pip and a badge of the 17th Dogra Regiment for each shoulder – I was a 2nd Lieutenant in His Majesty's Land Forces.

My first assignment was to the Training Battalion of the Dogras – the 10/17th Dogra Regiment that was based permanently at Jullunder in the Punjab. I was given charge of a platoon which consisted of four sections of seven *jawans*, as the soldiers were called. Each section was in the charge of a *naik* (a corporal) or a *havildar* (a sergeant). The mornings would be taken up with field exercises in the countryside around Jullunder, rather as we had done at Belgaum, with the major difference that we now had troops under our control. Afternoons were spent around a sand table carrying out military exercises in miniature on a scale model, map reading classes or attending lectures.

The regular army Officers treated emergency commissioned Officers, such as myself, with a certain amount of forbearance. Even the regular 2nd Lieutenants looked on us as a rather inferior, but unfortunately necessary, breed. This feeling is understandable when you remember that they had sweated for three years or longer to obtain a commission which we had, somehow or other, attained in four months.

By and large I got on well with the officers of the 10th Battalion and I enjoyed my stay in Jullunder very much. I had reasonably comfortable quarters, a long way superior to the barrack huts we had occupied at Belgaum. All meals were eaten in the mess, where breakfast and lunch were a rather moveable feast, with officers rolling up and departing at odd times. In contrast, dinner was a ceremonial affair in mess kit every evening. Our regimental mess kit comprised black dress trousers, white 'bum-freezer' mess jacket, with crested gold buttons and gold badges of rank on shoulder tabs, white cotton shirt with soft collar, black bow-tie and yellow cummerbund. One required a fresh and well-starched mess jacket every evening.

We would meet in the bar for pre-dinner drinks at 7.30pm for dinner at 8pm The head of the table was taken by the CO, or in his absence by the Senior Officer present. On his right sat the Second-in-Command and on his left the Adjutant. We lower mortals occupied the bottom end of the table and only addressed the higher echelon when spoken to.

The nearest town to Jullunder was Lahore, to which groups of young subalterns would repair at weekends to savour such high life and frivolity as was obtainable there – which wasn't much.

I had arrived at Jullunder at the beginning of June 1940 and in October of that year was told that I was now ready to join my battalion in Malaya. I was given a week's embarkation leave and moved down to Bombay to make final preparations and say goodbye to the office and such of my friends as were still around.

I don't remember much about that week, which must have been a fairly boisterous one, but I was eventually seen off one day towards the end of October from Ballard Pier heading east for Singapore.

CHAPTER SEVEN

MALAYA
NOVEMBER 1940 – NOVEMBER 1941

On the ship's arrival at Singapore, I was met by Bob Hyde, the Adjutant, who came on board as soon as the gangways were down, and contacted me through the public address system. Bob and I got on well from the start and he was very helpful in organising the transfer of my luggage from the ship to his jeep.

The drive from Singapore to the 2/17 Dogra Battalion HQ at Taiping took about eight hours. After we had crossed the causeway at Johore Baru, which separates Singapore island from the mainland, the road wound its way through one rubber plantation after another. Many of these rubber estates, and also the tin mines which comprised the two principal industries of Malaya, were managed by Scots, and I got to know a few of the rubber planters in the Taiping area very well indeed during the enjoyable year I was to spend there. Rubber estates occupied the centre of the country on either side of a central spine of hills, that stretched right up the peninsula, the highest peak being the Cameron Highlands. This latter was a hill station where wives and their families would spend some time each year to get away for a spell from the heat and humidity which pervaded at sea level throughout the year. Nearer the coasts to the east and west of the country, one found the tin mining industry.

During the drive north, we were given a glimpse of rubber tapping. The tappers, almost entirely Tamils, would shin up a rubber tree in a matter of seconds. This requires some agility and skill, as the trees are absolutely straight with a smooth bark and no footholds. On arrival at the top, the tapper would cut the bark with a special knife in a descending spiral round the tree leaving a channel about ¾" in width. Down this channel the liquid rubber or latex would trickle, eventually dripping into a cup fixed at the bottom of the tree. The cups had to be emptied into a large container at regular intervals.

Taiping is situated about 300 miles or two thirds of the length of Malaya from Singapore and closer to the West Coast than the East. The nearest town is Ipoh and the cities of Kuala Lumpur and Penang are conveniently located approximately equidistant from Taiping and within easy driving distance from it.

On arrival, I was installed in my quarters, which turned out to be a bungalow just round the corner from the mess, and shared by two subalterns, Peter Court

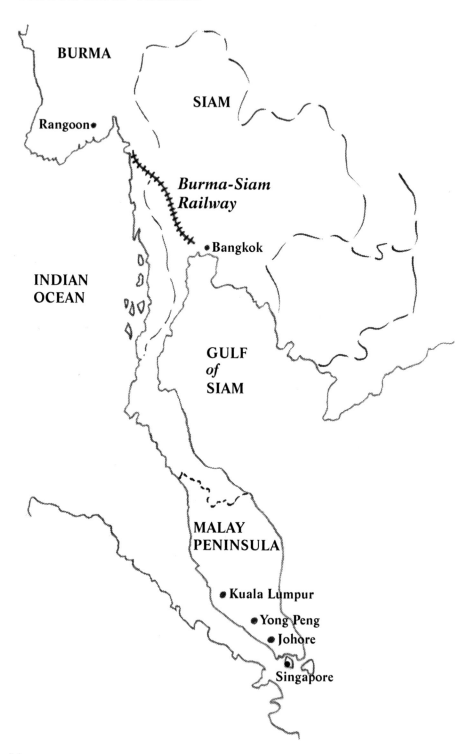

and Jack (Ben) Walton. At 7pm that evening all officers assembled in the mess in full mess kit and were introduced by Bob Hyde to the Colonel – S C Scott or 'Scotty' to his peers; the second-in-command 'Jumbo' Heaver (the Christian nomenclature speaks for itself), and the other officers, Major Jack Phelps, Captains Hector McLean, Bill Petty, Harvey Muir-Hardinge, Lieutenants Paul Mitchell, Owen Jenkins and Jack Downey. The only Emergency Commissioned Officers in the group were Muir-Hardinge, 2nd Lt. Peter Court and myself – all the others were regular army. I never quite worked out how Muir-Hardinge – M H to his friends – attained the rank of Captain in so short a time. I can only surmise, having known him for a year before the Japanese invasion, that it was earned by an indomitable spirit and a lot of bullshit. In short, he was a character. He hailed from Bombay where he had worked, I believe, as a car salesman before joining up. He was very helpful to me in showing me the ropes, helping me to integrate and to understand the set-up in Malaya. He was a complete extrovert and had little respect for authority, but he was a very good and fearless soldier as was later to be proved. Like most extroverts, he was very entertaining and had a fund of stories and anecdotes, some true, some probably untrue, at his command.

On some weekends, M H and I would set off in his jeep for either Penang or Kuala Lumpur, where he introduced me to the nightlife of these two cities. He also introduced me to one of his girl friends, Marjorie Bennetts, who lived with her family in the West End Hotel, Kuala Lumpur. Her younger sister, June, was brought along as a companion for me on these escapades, which suited me very well as she was in fact a lot more attractive than her sister. The Bennetts family were Australian and the father had a high powered job in the city, probably accounting for the fact that they could afford to live permanently in a suite in a first class hotel.

The unspoilt beauty of Penang in those days was breathtaking. This island, just ten minutes by ferry from the West Coast of Malaysia, is a paradise. Ferries used to ply every hour between Butterworth, on the mainland, and Georgetown, the capital of Penang. After a drive of about 1½ hours from Taiping we would leave the jeep at Butterworth and catch the next ferry. These ferries were invariably very crowded, and you had to literally squeeze yourself on if you arrived, as we usually did, at the last minute before departure. However, it was only ten minutes of discomfort pressed like a sardine between hordes of Malays and Chinese before you were disgorged at Georgetown.

Our base in Penang was the Eastern and Oriental Hotel (the E & O) in the centre of Georgetown, at that time the best hotel on the island. I understand that the new hotels which have sprung up in recent years bordering the many glorious beaches of silver sands that surround the island have now superseded it. The E & O was an old fashioned hotel by today's standards, and it had one peculiar feature in the enormous lounge with the domed roof. The shape of the roof played hell with the acoustics, and certain tables had a direct link-up soundwise with certain other tables at the other side of the room. The sometimes embarrassing effect of this was that persons talking in a whisper could be heard clear as a bell at another specific table some sixty feet distant at the opposite side of the room. The only saving grace was that it was difficult to pinpoint from which exact table the voices were coming.

Sundays in Penang were spent sunbathing on one of the beaches of pale sand backed by palm trees, with surfing in the crystal clear water before returning to the mainland by the last ferry for the drive back to Taiping.

Life in Taiping was not all beer and skittles, and we underwent quite rigorous training from Monday to Friday each week. The day started at 6am when the bugle sounded *reveille*. After a hurried shower and shave, there was an inspection of the troops in one's platoon, followed by an inspection of the lines – the troops' living quarters.

We used to get back to the mess around 8am. After breakfast there were planned military manoeuvres with the troops until lunchtime, and in the afternoons we had seminars and map-reading until 6pm. Assembly in the ante-room of the mess was at 7.30 for a cocktail before going in for dinner at 8pm. On Saturday nights everybody tended to let their hair down and I remember many rather boisterous – but never rowdy – nights in the mess. The bar would stay open until the last member had gone – either assisted or unassisted. On one occasion, the subalterns manhandled the C O's car – a small Volkswagen – into the mess and placed it on the billiard table where it was found next morning, much to the surprise of the CO. However, there were no serious recriminations.

Sunday morning was a ritual. We had the most fantastic natural pool within a couple of miles from our mess. This bathing spot was at the base of a cliff from the top of which a column of water fell from a great height into the water below. It was, in fact, a giant waterfall, the overflow from which spewed over the rocks surrounding the basin. The pool was about four feet deep and the cliff above it formed an overhang to provide an uninterrupted fall of water.

This spot was a popular venue on Sunday mornings as, after a heavy Saturday night in the mess, there is no more effective therapy than to sit in a pool of ice cold water and have your neck massaged by a massive weight of water dropping from 200 feet. Usually, a minute sitting in the pool directly below the waterfall was enough to effect a cure for the worst hangover – if the shock didn't kill you!

Life during the year I spent in Malaya was made the more enjoyable by the tremendous hospitality shown to us by the rubber planters and their wives on the neighbouring estates. Many a Sunday would see a group of us spending a day around their swimming pool and enjoying a delicious lunch of Nasi Goreng or curry. The local Tiger beer was better than most English bottled beers and was consumed in some quantity on these occasions.

CHAPTER EIGHT

THE CAMPAIGN
DECEMBER 1941 – FEBRUARY 1942

Unfortunately, our easy life in Malaya during 1941 was too good to last.

On December 7th, the Japanese attacked Pearl Harbour and shortly afterwards sank the *Prince of Wales* and the *Repulse* off the East Coast of Malaya, thereby not only entering the war but taking control of the Pacific.

From the Allies' point of view, the one redeeming feature was that these acts brought America into the war. The Pearl Harbour raid shook the High Command in Malaya to its foundations. The war in Europe had suddenly, at one stroke, been extended to the Far East for which they were ill prepared. Our battalion had been moved in the latter half of November to positions in a rubber plantation just north of Sungei Patani, close to the West Coast of Malaya and about 50 miles north of Taiping towards the Siamese border. At that time I was promoted to the rank of Captain.

On the night of December 7th, the Japanese began landing operations at Kota Bahru on the East Coast of Malaya, not far from the Siamese border and approximately opposite Sungei Patani on the other coast. In the early hours of December 8th, Singapore experienced its first air raid – but the seriousness of the situation was not appreciated by the people of Singapore who had always been told that the island was an impregnable fortress.

The reason for this belief stemmed from the topography of the peninsula to the north of the island, which was Malaya. This peninsula was long and narrow and stretched for four hundred miles to the Siamese border. It had a central spine of granite mountains rising to seven thousand feet, and four fifths of the country was covered with rubber plantations and dense tropical jungle. It was felt, therefore, by those responsible, that any attack would necessarily have to be sea borne, and this would have had no chance of success against the great 15-inch guns which faced out to the sea from the island. The surprise landing at Kota Bahru therefore came as a considerable shock and it was followed up by a massive air raid on Penang, which was evacuated shortly afterwards.

In the first few days of the war, the Japanese had bombed Singapore, secured the fall of Penang, landed troops, captured an airfield in the north and sunk two battleships, leaving Malaya without any substantial naval protection. In addition, in the hurried evacuation of Penang, hundreds of small craft were left intact for the Japanese to use for landings behind our own defensive positions.

By the end of the first week the 11th Division, of which our battalion was a part, had fallen back as the Japanese thrust inland from Kota Bahru. It found itself outflanked by swarms of Japanese riding bicycles at speed through the rubber plantations. These bicycles had been commandeered from the local Malays, and as the Japanese wore only shorts and singlets, they were indistinguishable from Malays, whom they resembled quite closely, to British eyes. These cycle groups by-passed the 'impenetrable jungle' moving at speed through dripping rubber plantations so silently that the defenders knew nothing of their presence till they were either attacked from the rear or cut off. Harvey Muir-Hardinge, who was cut off with a platoon of Dogras, blasted his way through the Japanese firing a tommy-gun from the hip and managed to link up with the rest of the battalion. He was subsequently awarded the MC.

The jungle and rubber plantations held no fear for the Japanese, but to the defenders struggling under the weight of heavy equipment in dripping vegetation and in blinding rain, it was unknown territory where the enemy could be anywhere and everywhere. Our defensive positions, in addition to being constantly outflanked, were subjected to regular aerial bombardment from the Japanese aircraft that already had control of the skies. After systematic attacks on RAF planes, many of them refuelling on the ground, the few that remained had been withdrawn to Singapore. In the period between Christmas Day and New Year's Day, the 11th Indian Division suffered a major attack by Japanese tanks supported by machine-gunning from the air and were forced to abandon their position on the Slim River with very heavy casualties. By January 1st, the enemy had overrun at least half of Malay, and whole pockets of troops had been cut off.

The first Japanese tanks came as a great surprise to the defenders who had not a single tank in Malaya. It had been felt that in jungle country tanks could not operate, but in fact the Japanese tanks moved with ease not only down the roads, but also between the rows of rubber trees. Air raids on our defensive positions became more frequent and were almost always in daylight, as happens when there is no fighter opposition. However, as far as possible the defenders had employed a scorched earth policy, and all tin mine dredgers, rubber store houses and other material which might have been of use to the enemy had been systematically destroyed and bridges blown up prior to evacuation.

During the rapid withdrawal down the peninsula, use was made of the planters' bungalows that were taken over as Battalion Headquarters or other administrative offices. These bungalows had been abandoned by their owners in great haste, the

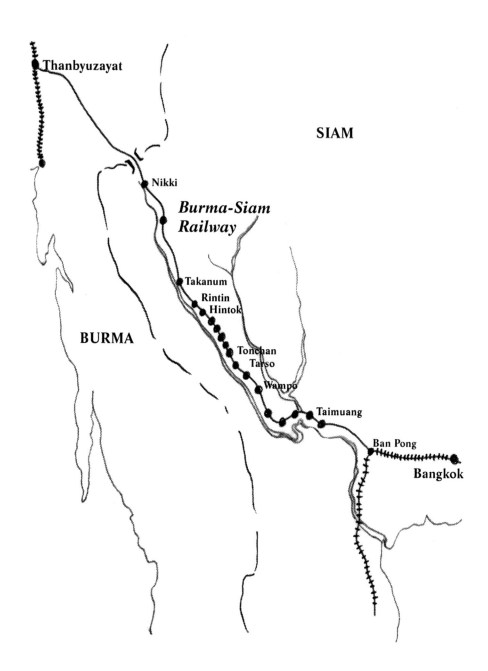

wives and children having been evacuated to Singapore by sea while the husbands fought alongside our troops as part of the Malay Volunteer Force. As the hard-pressed troops fell back from one ill-prepared position to another, worn out and hungry in the incessant rain, it was a further sadness to see these bungalows still fully furnished, some with family photographs which there had been no time to remove from the mantelpieces; bungalows so hastily evacuated that breakfast tables often carried remnants of the last hurried meal; bungalows thankfully occupied by us as a haven for a day or two, and later to be in the hands of the Japanese conquerors for the next three and-a-half years.

By mid-January, after a ferocious battle near the Muar River on the West Coast, in which only 800 out of 4000 Indian troops survived, the new defensive line that was drawn up stretched for 90 miles across the southern tip of Malaya and was barely 50 miles from Singapore.

The Causeway which joined Singapore to the mainland was crossed by some 30,000 beleaguered troops on the night of January 30th. Troops who had lost all interest in the war and were too tired to care about anything but sleep; troops who had been on the go for nearly two months, holding positions by day and withdrawing by night, against an enemy who held all the cards; troops who had been promised, right till the last, that air support was on its way – although for some weeks it had been known that Malaya had been written off by Whitehall as a lost cause. The promised air support had been diverted to the Russian front.

The last troops to cross the Causeway were what remained of the Argyle and Sutherland Highlanders, led by a piper playing the regimental march, who had fought all the way from the Siamese border and were all but decimated. When the last man had crossed the causeway, which was 1200 yards wide, it was blown with high explosives leaving a gap of about 60 feet. This presented no problem to the Japanese engineers and did little to slow the momentum of the advance.

Meanwhile, the city was being subjected to heavy artillery fire from the mainland, fires were raging in many streets, and the state of congestion had to be seen to be believed. Roads and squares, already crowded with military vehicles, became jammed with long streams of Chinese and Indian civilians heading for the east of the island – anywhere so long as it was in the opposite direction from the advancing Japanese.

To add to the confusion, there were thousands of dejected soldiers wandering about aimlessly, some stripped to the waist and some still wearing stinking clothes they had not changed for a long time. The enemy had captured the last remaining reservoir on the island, and what with burst mains due to bombing, water was becoming a real problem. I remember that by February 13th everyone accepted the fact that the battle had been lost. Japanese tanks were thundering down the Bukit Timan Road from a strategic hill they had captured. The whole city reeked with the smell of burning flesh, decaying bodies, smoke and cordite. It was somewhat surprising in this situation that we were still under instructions from Churchill, conveyed through General Percival, to fight to the last man and the last round and there must be no question of surrender.

The Alexandra Hospital to the north-west of the city, which was crammed to bursting point with wounded, was by this time in enemy hands and we subsequently heard frightful tales of atrocities carried out there by the Japanese. In spite of wearing Red Cross armbands, doctors and patients being prepared for operations were bayoneted to death in the theatre block of the hospital. A similar fate awaited patients in the wards who were taken away in groups of ten or so. Those who could not be moved were bayoneted in their beds.

At the docks, between air raids that had become more and more frequent, the last of the wives and children of civilians, plus thousands of key personnel, both military and civilian, were evacuated on Friday 13th February. They left in an armada of around fifty ships, ranging from naval sloops to outboard motor launches, heading for Java as a first base en route for Australia.

By February 14th, the scene was chaotic with fires raging in many streets and this, coupled with bomb damaged buildings, encouraged looting which had now become a norm. The Singapore River was a blaze of flame caused by a huge patch of burning oil from a bombed vessel in the mouth of the river which had floated upstream with the turn of the tide. This eventually reached the hundreds of sampans near the heart of the city and the Pinto Saigon Bridge, which crossed the river. The flames of the conflagration were so enormous they even reached the buildings on the banks of the river, setting them alight also.

With water, petrol, food and ammunition practically exhausted, General Percival approached the Japanese Headquarters under a white flag on the evening of Sunday 15th February, and I remember standing in Raffles Square listening to his announcement at 8.30pm that we had surrendered unconditionally.

Shortly after hearing this, many of us decided to make a break for it. We realised full well that we had far less chance of reaching Sumatra, and then Java, than those who had left officially on the 13th. But we still felt we had a chance if we could make Sumatra before dawn and hole up there until nightfall before finding a craft to take us across to Java – the eventual destination being Australia.

I found myself as the senior rank of a group of ten Officers and men in a sampan on the river to the south of the burning oil slick, as we pushed off from the bank at about 10pm. Each of us handled one oar, with five oars operating on each side of the sampan.

Unfortunately, in our urgency we had omitted to take two very important factors into consideration. The first was that none of us was a very experienced oarsman, and the second was that the tide had not yet turned, so we would be rowing against it as we travelled downstream towards the river estuary. Due to a combination of these factors, our progress was indeed slow during the first couple of hours, for although we must have travelled several miles in a lateral direction from one river bank to the other, we had attained no more than 500 yards in the required direction.

At this stage, it now being past midnight, I realised that we had no hope of making Sumatra before dawn. I also didn't fancy the idea of finding ourselves in the open strait in broad daylight – a sitting target for the Japanese fighter aircraft that would probably be scouring the strait from first light. I therefore announced to the others that if we hit the near bank of the river again, I was getting off and I strongly advised them to do the same. After some deliberation and argument weighing up the pros and cons, the others all voted in favour of carrying on and trying to make Sumatra, as the tide would be turning shortly.

Sure enough, we zigzagged for the umpteenth time into the near bank and, having failed to persuade any of the others to join me, I went ashore alone. The decision had not been an easy one. On the one hand was the possibility of escape with its attendant risks growing greater as the hours of darkness shortened; on the other, giving oneself up to an indefinite period of captivity. As it happened, I took the right decision, as I subsequently heard that all craft in the open strait between Singapore and Sumatra from first light on the Monday morning were machine gunned from the air – there were no survivors.

That Sunday night everybody in the city was physically exhausted and incapable of knowing whether to be relieved that the awful battle was over, or distressed that we were now prisoners in the hands of the Japanese for an indefinite period. All slept and slept as though dead in any place they could find to put their head down. Some were lucky enough to find a bed in Raffles and other hotels, some kipped down on the furniture in Robinsons department store, and some on the grass in the parks or even on the pavements – anywhere that involved as little walking as possible.

The guns had been silent since 8.30pm the previous evening and there was a deadly silence as I re-entered the city in the early hours of that Monday morning. The only sound was the crackle from the many fires that were still burning that sent up a luminous glow over the whole city. I found a place to kip down and slept.

Ronald Searle
Singapore 1942

64

Soon after dawn on Monday 16th February, the first Japanese troops entered the city and found themselves faced with an immediate and urgent problem. There were over a million civilians and more than eighty thousand hungry troops in the midst of the confusion that was Singapore. Looting was rampant, illuminated by fires burning everywhere, water was running to waste from burst mains, and wounded were lying dying in the streets. There was also the very real danger of an epidemic breaking out. Because the Japanese had gained their objective in very much quicker time than they had expected, they were not equipped to take over the civil administration of the city with all its inherent problems. It is now known that at the time of capitulation, their civil government officers were enjoying life in Bangkok – over a thousand miles to the north. In consequence, British doctors, nurses, firemen, water engineers and sanitary workers were ordered to remain at their posts until their Japanese counterparts arrived in order to restore some semblance of order to the city.

Singapore was in an unbelievable state on that Monday morning. I remember walking into Raffles Place and finding it packed with British, Australian and Indian soldiers squatting on the pavements, smoking and philosophically awaiting their future. Most units had become split up in the last hectic days of fighting. The Dogras had suffered heavy casualties, particularly the 3rd Battalion which was part of the force defending Kota Bahru at the time of the Japanese landings.

We were soon to learn that Indian Army Officers were to be segregated from their troops during internment. This was part of Japanese policy to break down discipline within units and to gain converts to the Indian National Army which had joined forces with the Japanese under the leadership of Subhas Chandra Bose as part of the 'Quit India' campaign against the British.

One of the first orders from the Japanese on entering the city was to pile arms, and enormous stacks of rifles, bayonets and pistols mushroomed in the centre of Raffles Place as troops added their arms to the mound surrounded by Japanese guards with fixed bayonets. The sight of a Gurkha Battalion performing this exercise is vivid in my memory. They had stacked their rifles and bayonets as ordered, but refused to part with their *kukris* – the curved knife from which they are never supposed to be parted. Eventually, of course, they were forced to remove their knives, and many of them had tears in their eyes as they reluctantly removed the scabbard containing the knife and piled it on top of the other arms.

The other order which had a devastating effect, was an announcement that all the thousands of patients in the General Hospital had to be evacuated within 24 hours, as the Japanese required the hospital for their own wounded. The military patients, many with serious injuries, had to be moved with great urgency to other buildings such as the Singapore Club or the Cricket Club, neither of which had any real facilities to look after them. The civilian patients who were able to walk were sent back to their homes, while those who were bedridden were sent to the Singapore Asylum from which the mental patients had already been despatched to an island off the coast of Singapore.

It was chaos.

CHAPTER NINE

END OF AN ERA
1942

The enormity of the disaster which had struck the Malay Peninsula took some time to penetrate people's minds. Approximately 140,000 British and Commonwealth troops had taken part in the campaign of which some 9000 were killed and about 130,000 taken prisoner, excluding the European civilians who were interned and the large numbers of the local population killed by bombing and shelling.

This had been accomplished in just over two months by a Japanese force of some 55,000 men, of whom only 3,500 were killed.

Many reasons have been put forward to explain away why more was not done to slow down the pace of the Japanese advance. There is no doubt that an attack, if it came, was expected to come from the sea and not from the north. Certainly the gun emplacements on Singapore island were aligned against a sea borne attack. The RAF fighter planes at the various bases in Malaya at the time of the Japanese invasion were outmoded and vastly inferior to the enemy planes, and in any event most of them were destroyed on the ground in the first few days by Japanese bombers. Therefore, the advance was made that much easier against an army lacking air support. The deployment of our troops across the breadth of the country meant that defence in depth was impossible, and created a pattern of Japanese infiltration behind our line of defence necessitating regular withdrawals to new defensive positions overnight. Furthermore, it was thought that the Japanese would use the rubber plantations for their advance much more than in fact they did, and the possibility of them advancing down the roads and rubber plantations in tanks never seemed to have occurred to anybody. Anti-tank gun emplacements on the roads, therefore, were sadly lacking.

After the fall of Penang in the early days, the Japanese inherited a fleet of small craft that was not destroyed, and they were able to use these to advance down the West Coast and to get behind our lines. There was no naval opposition. The loss of the *Prince of Wales* and the *Repulse* at the outset of the war was a bitter blow. Obviously, in hindsight, no air or naval support was to be forthcoming, and Malaya and Singapore were to be left to flounder with the resources at their command – Churchill was to give precedence to the war in Europe. The only support provided was in manpower in the form of the 18th Division, which was landed in Singapore in the last week of the war. This Division was composed of unblooded young soldiers who had never fired a shot in anger. They were no match for the seasoned Japanese soldiers, but fortunately for them they had little fighting to do before being scooped up into the bag with the rest of us.

Although all the above facts played their part in bringing about the worst military disaster in British history, there was another more human factor.

For many years there had been friction between the military command and the civil administration. The former were concerned with putting Malaya into an efficient state of defence, and the latter with increasing the country's production for export of the raw materials, rubber and tin. These two diametrically opposed aims led to inevitable clashes over the best use of European manpower. The civil authorities were eager to use the available Europeans to help increase the production of tin and rubber, while the military pressed for the mobilisation of the volunteer forces which formed a substantial part of the Army's paper strength. The civil authorities won in the end, as it was considered vital to give priority to the claims of industry in war-torn Europe.

The European planters and tin miners, therefore, carried on very much as usual with only sporadic training as a volunteer force. This highlighted the difference between European civilians in Malaya and the soldiers of units who arrived there after the outbreak of war in Europe. The picture of the whisky-swilling planter, as depicted by Somerset Maugham, is well known but perhaps not fully justified. The climate of Malaya controlled the time and pace of work, which started early and finished around 5pm. There were sports at the clubs before the sun set around 6.30pm every day of the year. After changing clothes, the men would either stay on drinking in the club or go home to their big old-fashioned bungalows with wide verandas.

The war-time conscripts launched into this environment immediately resented being made to feel strangers in a community that played tennis, danced and drank *stengahs* as if the war in Europe didn't exist. For the other ranks, social distinctions and low pay limited their scope for enjoyment. Eating out was a rare experience and entertainment was restricted to local bars and cinemas.

The resentment felt by other ranks is typified by a story told by a Sergeant who, finding himself in Singapore in the confusion of the last few days, entered Raffles Hotel. He found the bar area packed with Officers, mostly in khaki, but some in full mess kit. There were few women, but those present wore evening dresses and were outnumbered ten to one. The orchestra was playing, and nobody looking at the scene could have guessed that a war was on.

The Sergeant headed for the bar, but was stopped on the way by some British

Banzai! First days, Singapore 1942

16 Feb 94

Staff Officers who called him a scruffy devil and ordered him out before he was thrown out. And this was a man who had fought his way down the peninsula and who was trying to get a drink in the last few days before capitulation.

On hearing this story, one can understand the resentment felt by the troops.

A poem, written by an anonymous but humble member of our forces, vividly expresses the ennui and bitterness of those garrisoning the outposts of an Empire upon which the sun was rapidly setting.

MALAYAN MALADY

'Oh! How I hate this tropic land
It's burning heat and yellow sand.
I hate the morning's burning light,
I hate the suffocating night,
The long and listless afternoon
And then the dark that comes too soon,
The frangipani's cloying smell
And all the other smells as well.

I hate the food, I hate the drink,
I hate the all pervading stink
Of squalid, crowded Chinatown
With bodies yellow, black and brown,
The petty spite, the stupid brag,
The social tripe in the local rag,
The endless chatter, the vapid bleat
Of the girls of the local fishing fleet.

The tropic moonlight leaves me cold
With all its myriad stars untold,
The black Sumatra's sudden rain,
The tom-toms maddening refrain,
The rubber trees, unlovely whores
With obscene scars and running sores,
And whining mozzies round my net
Have failed to fascinate me yet.

The futile trek from flic to hop,
The floorshows on the Cathay top
The naval blokes in portly rig
Who execute a stately jig,
The army subs with weak moustache,
The RAF so short of cash,
The shrivelled dames so hard to please;
From all of these I crave release.

The tuan besars a motley crew,
The Towkays, Datos, Tenghus too,
The curry tiffs, the evening pahits,
The blaring bands, the shaded lights,
The Colonels with the Majors' wives,
The smug intrigues, the double lives,
The lovelies at the Bomber Ball –
By Jesus Christ, I hate them all!
Yes, how I hate this tragic land
Of burning heat and yellow sand,

The ceaseless waste of precious time,
The Tuans mainly past their prime,
The Chinese ladies neat and trim,
The apathetic boredom grim
In all its aspects, fair and bland,
God! How I hate this tropic land!'

CHAPTER TEN

CHANGI
FEBRUARY 1942 – AUGUST 1942

By Tuesday morning, we had learnt that civilians were to be interned in Changi jail, while British and Australian troops would be interned in the Military Barracks at Changi, along with Indian troops who would be segregated in a separate camp.

By 10am several thousand civilian men, women and children had been lined up in the blazing sun for the march to the jail. Simultaneously, the gigantic military contingent was being lined up for the 15-mile march to Changi Military Barracks. Every man carried on his back what remained of his worldly possessions and these, as it turned out, had to last for a very long time. Basic rations were transported in trucks, which followed the convoy. There was only one reservoir that supplied water to the whole of Singapore Island and, with the sudden increase in population, water was at a premium. Each unit was allowed to take one water truck and one truck of such food as had remained at the time of capitulation.

Needless to say, neither the water nor the food lasted very long.

So far as the basic necessities of life were concerned, one's worldly possessions at this stage depended on how successful one had been in the looting which had been widespread in the hours prior to the Japanese entry into Singapore. Some of the British and Australian troops had managed to amass a considerable quantity of edible goodies such as tinned food and personal possessions such as watches which could always be converted into cash. Many of us who had more than we could physically carry on the march were able surreptitiously to heave a sack or two on to the trucks which trundled along at walking pace behind us, and whisk them off in the confusion that prevailed on arrival at Changi Barracks.

We were a mournful and bedraggled procession as we traversed the 15 miles along the road to Changi under the blazing sun, our clothes soaked in sweat, with the Japanese guards walking alongside us and bashing with rifle butt anyone who tended to lag behind. Looking back on it now, Changi was a blissful interlude, in the respect that we arrived at a military cantonment, with huts already built for us to sleep in at the end of the march, by comparison with what was in store for many of us in Thailand, where we had to build our own in the jungle.

But that comes later.

On arrival we were assembled in the square and given a pep talk by the Japanese

Commandant. He told us, through an interpreter, that we were now prisoners of the Imperial Japanese Army, that we would be well treated as long as we obeyed the rules, but that anyone who was caught either trying to escape, or operating a radio, would be shot. He then produced a load of propaganda enumerating the allied losses in the war to date. It appeared we had lost all the Pacific islands between Australia and Malaya and, furthermore, the war was going very badly for the Allies in Europe. We were told – which turned out to be true – that of the fifty-eight ships that had left Singapore on February 13th, aerial bombing or machine gunning had sunk forty-six of them. So the point was forcefully made that there was no future in trying to escape now that Nippon was in complete control of the air and sea surrounding the islands. He finished his address with the words: "Tojo Number one, Churchill Number Ten!"

Changi Military Barracks were spread over a large area and were allocated into sections, each section being about a mile away from its neighbour. This made it possible for the Japanese to separate the enormous number of prisoners into smaller groups, each with its own independent administration.

A certain amount of free movement was permitted between sections in the initial stages, and groups of prisoners would march under a Japanese guard to visit neighbouring camp sites. Along the route, sentries were posted whom we had to salute as we passed them. Among these sentries were a number of Indian soldiers and NCOs, the majority of them Sikhs, who had joined the Indian National Army (INA) after capitulation. Some of these had joined voluntarily in order to have an easier life than they would have had as Prisoners of War. Some joined as a result of indoctrination, at which the Japanese were past masters. Others were forced into it against their will by starvation and torture. Those in the two former categories would take sadistic pleasure in beating up British Officers on the grounds that they considered the salute of the Officer to be sloppy. This retribution took the form of rifle-butt bashing as vigorous as that carried out by the Japanese sentries. Some of those, however, who had been forced into the INA against their will, felt embarrassed by the situation in which they found themselves. I remember one Sikh who, on being saluted by one of his own ex-Officers, bowed his head rather than return the salute, demonstrating his sense of shame.

Our life at this stage centred on a very few priorities. First was food, which consisted of boiled rice and vegetable stew thrice daily. These were collected in tubs from the cookhouse, where our cooks had produced what they called rice, but which was more like glue, and another tub of watery vegetables. The members of the camp, at the call "Grubs up!" would proceed to queue at the bamboo-slatted table, situated at one end of the square, on which these delectable morsels reposed.

Prisoners queueing for their rice.
Ronald Searle, Changi May 1942.

The ration was one scoop of rice and one ladle of vegetable stew per head, which was served out to the queue by two cooks, one serving the rice and one the stew, supervised by an Officer. After all the men had been served, the Officers lined up and were given their ration. Anything that was left in the tubs after everybody had been served was known as *leggis*, which means 'more' in Malay. *Leggis* were collected by a numerical system known as your *leggi* number, to ensure that *leggis* were allocated on a fair roster system. On the odd occasion, our hosts presented us with a few carcasses of meat to add to the stew. This meat was invariably 'off', to put it mildly, and was certainly unfit for human consumption.

We had among us members of every profession and trade, including butchers and health inspectors, and the latter had the responsibility of passing verdict on the state of the carcasses. After dissection by the butchers, the health inspectors would consign most of the carcasses, which they considered beyond consumption, to the bonfire, watched by thousands of ravenous eyes. Those pieces that passed the test were cut into cubes of greenish meat which, after stewing, had the vilest taste imaginable and smelt of sewage. We knew, of course, that it was of vital importance to our survival to get that meat – however foul-tasting – into our stomachs and hold it down. This often took a lot of will power.

I had made up my mind to eat anything in order to have the maximum intake of vitamins and protein. Meat, whether horse, dog or cat, snake, frogs, snails, and the green leaves from any plant from which our vegetable stew was made, all went down the hatch. A common joke was about the weevils, always present in the rice. One chap would say "Hey, I've got weevils in my rice!" His mate would reply, "Lucky you, getting all that extra protein."

However, we needed more than extra proteins from weevils, and in this respect some were more fortunate than others. The period of free looting in the last few days in Singapore had brought to the more adventurous a harvest of goods now worth their weight in gold. The Japanese loved any Western trinkets, such as watches and pens, and a good trade in these was carried out in the early days in Changi. Much haggling took place and also much duplicity. A Japanese sentry would catch sight of a pen in a prisoner's shirt pocket and say "Parker ka?" The answer to this had to be in the affirmative as the name was the criterion as far as the Japanese were concerned.

"Ah so ka!" the Japanese would say, although the inscription on the pen rarely said 'Parker', but as he couldn't read English it didn't really matter. The prisoner would then strike a hard bargain to get the maximum possible price for what was probably a worthless pen. The same procedure was adopted for watches, where Rolex was the magic word.

After some time, we realised that some of the Japanese knew what the Parker and Rolex trademarks looked like, and we were no longer able to get away with passing off inferior goods. By this time, however, we had found among our motley crew an engraver who was able to scratch out the name Parker or Rolex on any pen or watch well enough to deceive the Japanese, to whom Parker was Number One and Rolex was Number One.

The money raised from the Japanese in this way helped to provide the necessities of life in the way of food that we needed to supplement our diet. Contacts with the Malays near the camp were set up, and cash could be converted into such essentials as eggs, bananas and groundnuts, thereby staving off the onslaught of the dreaded beri-beri, which was already beginning to manifest itself amongst us inmates, due to lack of vitamin B in our diet.

Beri-beri was caused by an excess of fluid in the body, and the initial symptoms were a swelling around the ankles and the legs below and around the knee. A thumb pushed into the shin-bone of a sufferer from the complaint left an indentation which remained after the thumb had been withdrawn, the flesh not springing back after depression. Such holes could be up to an inch deep. If this illness is not arrested it can, and did in many cases, result in cardiac beri-beri where the heart, being starved of vitamins, just stops. You could be talking to a man and he would suddenly keel over, and that was it.

Two other very uncomfortable complaints caused by our diet were what became known throughout the camps of Malaya and Thailand as 'Rice Balls' and 'Happy Feet'.

'Rice Balls' does not, as you might imagine, refer to the Japanese delicacy of which they are so fond, but to an effect on the scrotum caused by lack of vitamin B2. The first symptom was an itch, which almost drove one mad, as the more you scratched the worse the itch became. The second stage was a splitting of the skin of the scrotum, which would then peel off large areas of the genitals extending well down the inner thigh. This left these areas very red, extremely painful and sticky and of course a target for infection. I doubt if any prisoners escaped 'Rice Balls' to a greater or lesser degree during their internment. It was simple: we ate rice, we got 'Rice Balls'. QED.

'Happy Feet' was also the result of a vitamin deficiency, but fortunately it was not nearly so widespread. The symptoms were stabs of burning pain in the soles of the feet, and the immediate reaction was to plunge the feet into cold water. This, however, failed to relieve the pain – the water simply felt like ice and the stabs continued. The few who suffered from 'Happy Feet' went downhill very quickly and you could see them ageing almost before your eyes. They became old and

desperate men as the flesh literally dropped off their bones in a very short space of time – similar to victims of the worst attacks of dysentery.

What made prisoners most furious was the fact that they knew the Japanese had vast quantities of drugs at their disposal, as well as all those they had captured from us. They must surely have had hundreds of thousands of vitamin B tablets, which would have been a godsend for all those suffering from beri-beri, 'Rice Balls' and 'Happy Feet'. However, the numerous representations that were made by the Senior Officers of the many camps throughout the country during the period of our internment were all turned down flat by the Japanese Commandants of these camps. They even refused to allow us a ration of rice polishings from their own rice, which was useless to them, thereby condemning thousands of men to endure the discomfort and misery of weeping flesh in a very sensitive area of the body. To all the requests for drugs, whether quinine for malaria, emetin for dysentery – which was almost as prevalent as 'Rice Balls' – or vitamin B tablets, the answer was always the same, "Ashita", which means tomorrow – which in reality meant never. In many cases, the reply was less polite – a severe bashing with a rifle-butt for the individual who was courageous enough to ask.

The Japanese policy on drugs was known to the prisoners throughout the camps as 'Jap Bastardry'. Our own doctors, in spite of the lack of drugs, did wonders with the little they had at their disposal. Epsom salts was the great standby for all stomach complaints, including dysentery. For external wounds such as those frequently obtained when out on working parties, and for skin diseases such as scabies or ringworm, the standard treatment was an application of what we called 'Hell Fire' ointment – a mixture of sulphur and mosquito cream. The effect on a patient when this mixture was applied to his scrotum caused not a little concern among those in the queue awaiting similar treatment, and did little to bolster their morale, to put it mildly.

From the first days in Changi, and progressively throughout our incarceration, personal physical and mental well being became an obsession with most POWs, and they were prepared to go to great lengths and take considerable risks to achieve the former. After we moved north to Thailand, the situation became even more urgent and night forages outside the confines of the camp wire to contact local villagers were frequent. We all realised that to stay alive every individual had to augment his rice ration with food high in vitamins and protein content. Such foods as bananas, groundnuts, gula sugar, duck eggs, etc, were invaluable, but these could only be obtained from the villagers in exchange for local currency.

Some of us started off our POW life with more ready cash than others, but eventually it had to run out. When that happened it was necessary to sell one's personal possessions such as a watch, a ring, English or American cigarettes, or articles of clothing to either the Korean guards or the local Thai villagers.

As time rolled on, those who started with the least in worldly goods eventually ran out of both cash and possessions that could realise cash. In this sort of situation, a black market usually thrives, and prison camps in Thailand were no exception. Those who were still flush with money were prepared to sell foodstuffs on credit, there being no other option, to those less fortunate. Many POWs built up large debts over the years, knowing that without the extra vitamins and protein, they would be unlikely to see the end of the war anyway.

The prices charged were fantastic by any standards, and calculated in Straits dollars. The Straits dollar was worth at that time 2/8d (the equivalent of about 13p in 1982). Eggs cost Straits $40 each, butter was St $400 per pound, and powdered milk St $650 per tin. Payment was made by signing chits to be settled after the war was over.

The justification for the exorbitant prices charged was threefold. Firstly, the risk involved in venturing out through the wire at night, without being spotted by the Japanese, to make purchases from the local Thais, knowing full well the sort of reprisals that would be taken if one was caught. Secondly, there was the ever-increasing difficulty in preserving the IOUs over the years, as our clothing got less and less, and the Japanese regular searches became consequently that much easier. Thirdly, there was the distinct possibility that either the buyer or the seller would not survive the period of incarceration, in which event the contract became null and void.

An interesting anecdote in this connection concerns two IOUs in the form of cheques I had issued, one to an Australian other rank, and one to a British officer. Both were for around £200, which was a considerable amount in those days. I had arrived back in India after the war in the spring of 1946, following six months leave, to resume work at Finlays. Some time after I got back, – it must have been towards the end of 1946 or early 1947 – I received a letter from my bank in Scotland, a very staid establishment indeed. It stated, with thinly veiled astonishment, that they had received a visit from a very rough-looking individual, speaking with a strong antipodean accent, who had presented them with an extraordinary document. This took the shape of a filthy, crumpled piece of paper made out in the form of a cheque and practically illegible, but bearing my signature. The bank, with customary scrupulousness, asked for instructions, and I replied by return cable requesting them to honour the document that had been preserved throughout by the Australian POW.

About the same time I received a letter from the British officer, saying that he

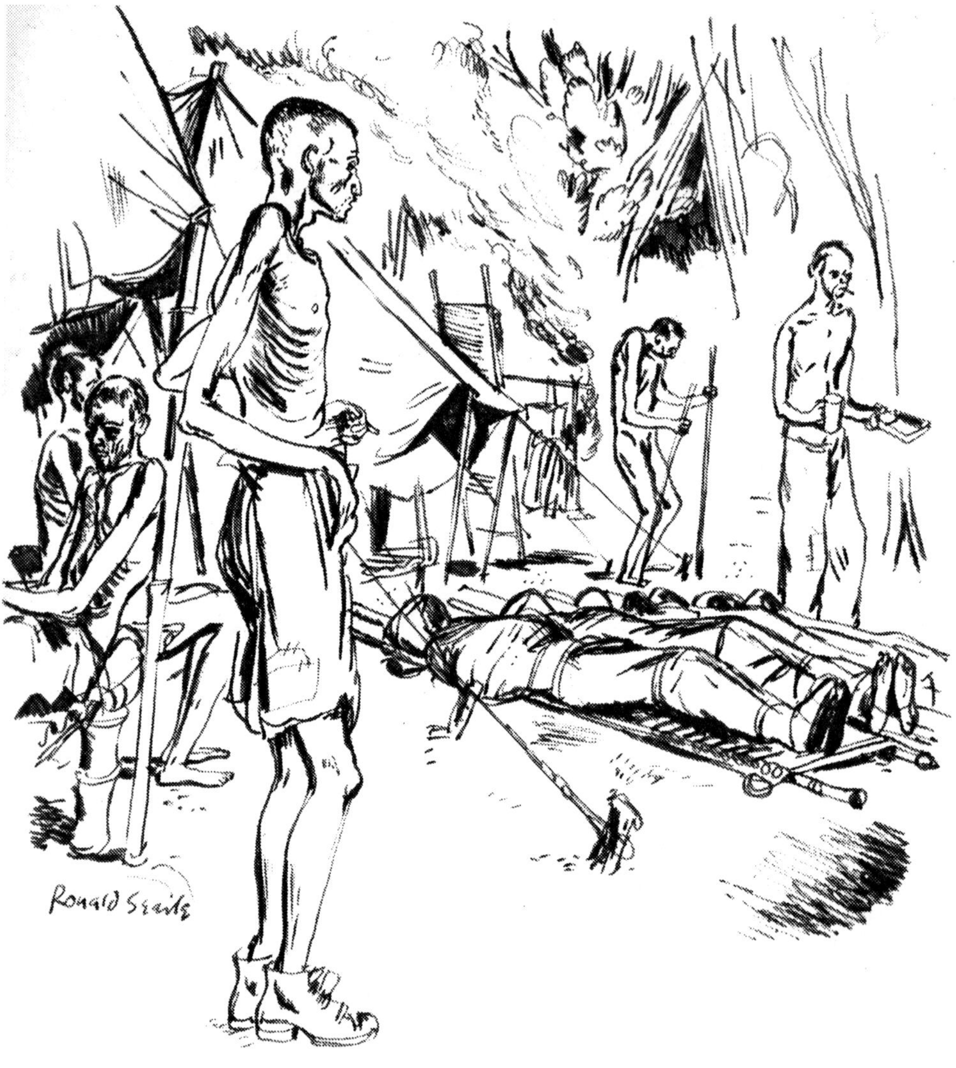
Ronald Searle

Cholera lines. – Thai-Burma Railway.

Cholera [illegible] reduced the population of slave camps to 50% in a few weeks.

had lost my IOU but reminding me of the amount and asking me to settle. The agreement had always been that IOUs would only be honoured if they were kept and presented, so I'm afraid I felt no moral obligation in this respect and wrote and told him so. I heard nothing further.

The afflictions induced by malnutrition naturally got progressively worse, and in retrospect I look back on Changi as a rest haven by comparison with what came later in Thailand. The speedy adaptation to POW life was made easier firstly by the inherent optimism of the British and Australian troops. We firmly believed that we would be freed within six months, and this period was progressively extended to a further six months after the first period had expired. This was the maximum our minds could endure, and had we known at the outset that the period would extend to three and-a-half years, I doubt very much if some of those who survived would, in fact, have done so.

This inherent optimism in the troops was fed and nurtured by rumours that were abundant throughout our internment, right from the early days. They were known as 'bore-holes' because they usually originated while troops were squatting next to each other above the latrines. These were holes bored into the ground to a depth of about 10 feet, and the construction of these was always our first task every time we moved camp. Very soon they had millions of maggots writhing at the bottom. They had no seats of course – you squatted Indian fashion – and there were no partitions, just twenty to thirty holes about eighteen inches in diameter in a long line surrounded by woven palm *attap* walls and a roof thatch. This was the one place where you were away from the Japanese and could talk without fear of being overheard, and many fantastic stories were invented by wishful thinking minds while squatting on the bog in the prison camps.

The second factor that contributed to our chance of survival was the natural sense of humour of the troops. They would always see the funny side of any incident, however bizarre, and would often risk a bashing from the Japanese guards by baiting them just to raise a laugh from the assembled congregation.

A typical example of this was when negotiations for the sale of a watch or pen were taking place. Knowing that the Japanese understood little or no English apart from a few set phrases, the seller would say something like, "Hurry up, you horrible little gold-toothed ape and buy this completely worthless watch."

This, needless to say, caused great amusement among the spectators.

The third factor that helped the morale considerably, was the ability to adapt and make the best of things no matter how adverse the conditions. We made our own entertainment from among the wealth of talent in our midst. Amongst our numbers, and this applied to all the camps we occupied in ensuing years, were to be found representatives of any profession, trade or sport you could think to mention. In the evenings it was always possible to find someone to volunteer to give a talk on his job or hobbies, and the amount of information gained in this way about the other man's job was a source of constant interest to us all. After a hard day's labour, it was relaxing to sit down of an evening and just listen – it also kept one's mind off other things. We had talks on such diverse subjects as 'Good Wines and How to Recognise Them' and 'Acquaplaning'.

We also had an international contract bridge player who was happy to run classes for enthusiasts, and we had a keen mountaineer, who was in fact to be a member of the successful Everest expedition led by Sir John Hunt in 1954. His name was Charles Wylie and he was at that time a Captain in the 2nd Gurkhas.

No group would be complete without some members of the acting profession and many plays and sketches were staged in the evenings during the period we spent in Changi. At this early stage in our confinement, we could still obtain makeshift stage props and colour for the backdrops painted by budding artists in our midst. The plays were very professionally done on a proper stage erected by our carpenters with a proper curtain. Some of the 'girls' looked most realistic and also attractive – I never found out how the female attire or the make-up was obtained. The popular TV show *It Ain't Half Hot, Mum* gives an idea of the type of show that was most popular with the troops, although straight plays were also produced. A contingent of Japanese would attend most of these shows and they seemed to get some amusement out of our antics, which was surprising, as they couldn't understand a word that was said.

Another pastime of an evening was a singsong. It is a fact that whenever you get a group of British Tommies together, they will eventually burst into song. Many an evening, when some of our spirits were a bit low, perhaps due to a lack of encouraging bore-holes, they were lifted by a rousing singsong of all the popular songs of World Wars I and II which fairly raised the rafters, or *attap* roofs. These singsongs were not popular with the Japanese who found it difficult to comprehend how we could exude such a carefree attitude in view of the serious plight in which we found ourselves. It also infuriated them that the constant propaganda that they fed to us did not appear to be having the desired effect. How could people who had just been told, "The Allies are losing the war" and "You will never see your families again", behave in such a manner? It was indeed a puzzlement to the Japanese.

Living together in such close proximity taught us one very important lesson, and this was self-discipline. This manifested itself in many ways. It required rigid self-discipline to ensure that the ground around the bore holes did not get fouled in

Thai-Burma Railway — lunch, along the jungle track on my to ____

Ronald Searle.

order to restrict as far as possible disease carrying flies – not always an easy matter if you were suffering from a bout of dysentery. Those put in charge of dishing out our rations also required self-discipline to ensure that the small quantity of food allocated to us was shared equally between all of us, including themselves, to give everyone an equal chance of survival.

Also, each one of us had the daily task of allocating the limited water available between slaking one's thirst, washing one's mess tin and eating utensils, washing oneself and one's teeth, and filling the glass bottle that always accompanied one to the latrines. Paper was much too valuable and scarce a commodity to throw down a bore-hole. Its many uses included writing IOUs, keeping a diary, and as cigarette paper for the indigenous tobaccos. Besides, in these conditions, we found water a much cleaner method and with practice became quite proficient in its use at the bore-hole. There was a knack in avoiding getting either your boots full of water or your hand full of something worse! Whenever you saw someone crossing the square carrying a glass bottle of water, you knew invariably where he was going.

Many men brought books into the camp, and the most valuable of these was the Bible but not, I'm afraid, for ecclesiastical reasons. The smokers amongst us were able to obtain tobacco from the local Malays. This came in bundles wrapped in newspaper and was about the size of a bundle of wool. Before smoking it, it had first to be teased out and the long strands wrapped in newspaper to make a cigarette. Ten times stronger than Virginia tobacco, it was known by various names, 'Hags Bush' and 'Sikhs Beard' being the most common. The paper of the cigarette was stuck together with spit and on lighting it and puffing invariably burst into flames at the end farthest from the mouth. The smoke caused you to cough and splutter until you got used to it. It had its repercussion at the end of the war when real Virginia cigarettes were dropped into the prison camps in Thailand by parachute – one of the luxuries we had been looking forward to for three and-a-half years – and we couldn't taste them!

To revert to the Bible, it was soon discovered that its thin pages made an ideal wrapping for 'Hags Bush'. Stocks of newspaper were quickly used up and newspapers were of course unobtainable, but in any case the thin paper of the Bible was infinitely superior. On puffing at a cigarette made with a Bible page, it burst into a much smaller conflagration at the end than one made with newsprint. The owner of a Bible had a veritable gold mine as he could sell the thousands of pages to the addicts page by page and obtain cash for food over a considerable period of time.

Teeth suffered badly as a result of the rice diet and there was little one could do to retard their deterioration, apart from regular cleaning. This was accomplished by applying charcoal from burnt wood with the finger to the teeth and gums.

Shaving was a ritual carried out less and less, as stocks of razor blades ran out. Many POWs, however, continued to have a semblance of a shave for a long time on their last few blades by honing them on the inside of a broken bottle. Shaving without soap and with a blunt blade was a painful process, but it was possible to remove the worst of the beard.

In August 1942, six months after the fall of Singapore, the Japanese announced that those POWs who were fit were being sent north to Siam where conditions would be much easier and less crowded than in Changi. The general feeling about this announcement was one of relief in that any change in surroundings was welcome, and perhaps in Siam there would be more opportunity for escape than there was on Singapore Island surrounded as we were by water on four sides.

What we did not know was that with typical Japanese duplicity we were being sent on the long and terrible trek to build what became known as the Siamese railway of death. Those who remained in Changi, which included all civilian POWs and all Indian troops, turned out to be the more fortunate ones, as those who were sent to the work camps in Siam were to die in their thousands before the railway was completed.

The Siamese party included all reasonably fit British, Dutch and Australian troops and included the Malay Volunteer Regiment. I have not previously mentioned the presence of Dutch POWs in our camps. These men were originally captured on neighbouring islands of the Dutch East Indies and subsequently transported to Singapore after capitulation.

· Ronald Searle ·
Singapore .

A 'beating up'
for failing to salute a Japanese

CHAPTER ELEVEN

One day in August 1942, I found myself one of a large contingent marching from Changi to Singapore railway station. Everyone carried what he could on his back and ditched the rest. We were on our way to construct a railway through the jungle of Siam, now Thailand, linking up Malaya to the south with Burma to the north – approximately 500 miles of track.

On arrival at the station, we were divided into groups of thirty to thirty-five and lined up opposite a goods train of covered wagons with sliding doors at each side. Each group was allotted a wagon and ordered at bayonet point to load the baggage first, which almost completely covered the floor. After that we all piled in to what was to be our residence for the next four days and four nights. I remember there was insufficient room for anyone to lie down and very little room to move at all.

Twice a day the train stopped at pre-arranged stations where food was dished out – rice and vegetable stew. Drinking water was not provided and we had to make do with what we had in our water bottles. However, it was possible to buy fresh fruits at the stops. The train rattled on through days of blistering sunshine when the metal trucks became extremely hot, the sides and the roof being too hot to touch, and only those in the middle of the trucks opposite the sliding doors got the benefit of cool, fresh air.

At night it became positively cold, and the metal sweated. We were glad then of our close proximity to keep warm. It was impossible to sleep in the welter of legs, bodies, angular baggage and knobbly packs. Not only was drinking water short but also only at the rarest intervals could one get a splash of water to wash oneself, let alone our clothes. Sweating, cramped, unshaven, bleary-eyed and dirty, we soon presented a shocking appearance – and smell!

In addition to the stops for food, the train also stopped for short breaks for the convenience of the driver and the guards, but otherwise if we were caught short we had to answer the call of nature by opening the sliding doors. This was a hazardous – not to say embarrassing – exercise for the performer, and not too pleasant for the rest of us in the truck with the wind blowing inwards from the moving train.

About midday on the fifth day we halted at the station of Bam Pong and we were ordered to get out. We staggered from the trucks into a land of jungle where the rain was pouring down in a solid sheet. In spite of this, it was a great relief to get out of the cramped conditions. A phrase was coined from Churchill's famous words, "Never have so many travelled so far in so few".

Shouldering our kit, we were lined up on the road outside the station. The Japanese had to satisfy themselves that we were all present, and after endless waiting, endless shouting and argument, count and recount, they appeared to be satisfied and we marched off through the shabby little town and along a jungle track for several miles to a large transit camp.

The camp covered an area of about 250 yards square situated between the railway and the road and surrounded by a bamboo fence. Huts occupied most of the camp area – flimsy structures of bamboo thatched with *attap* – each about twenty-five feet wide at ground level with a sloping roof that came down on each side to about two feet above the ground.

Inside the huts there was a central passageway with split bamboo slats down each side. On to these slats, with our packs as pillows, we laid our weary bodies. The huts must have been about eighty yards long and were very dark inside, the only light getting in from the openings at either end. Such kit as we had was stored at the back of our space on the slats, and some used a piece of string stretched between the poles of the hut frame to hang clothes. Dust filtered down constantly from the *attap* roofs, and in the concave underside of the bamboo slats lurked an army of bed bugs. These appeared to sleep during the day, but ventured forth at night for their midnight feast of blood provided by the recumbent bodies above them. Ants were everywhere and myriads of mosquitoes reposed in the darkness of the roof. These combined factors made sleep a little difficult.

One hut was allocated as a hospital but it was exactly the same as the others in size and construction, and in here our doctors did what they could with the little available to them for the afflicted ones. The latrines lay in a line not more than a few yards distance along the bottom ends of the huts. They consisted of bore-holes to which we were becoming accustomed, but their location made the bottom ends of the huts nearly uninhabitable because of the stench and the clouds of bluebottles permanently droning over them. However, the huts were so crowded that the bottom ends had to be used.

There was no source of water in the camp and the nearest well was about a quarter of a mile along the road. This necessitated going outside the camp, past the Japanese guardhouse at the entrance. This could only be done under guard in organised parties that were necessarily small due to shortage of containers. Unfortunately, there was no tank into which water could be poured from the buckets used for trips to the well. There was no area allocated for washing and one had to carry out one's ablutions in narrow spaces between the huts. A bucket of water would wash about a dozen men if they were economical in its use. As the fit men were mostly out on working parties all day, there were too few remaining in camp to fetch sufficient water for the working parties to use on their return from a day's toil. Sometimes it was possible to bathe in a ditch or pond outside the camp, but washing on return from work was out of the question. Because of this, skin diseases caused by dirt such as scabies became progressively more serious.

It is difficult to remember day-to-day incidents, or even the sequence of events in the three years spent in many camps up and down Thailand before, during and after constructions of the railway. The actual building of the railway took about a year of the three years we spent in Thailand. The period before was taken up in the construction of transit camps in the jungle along the route the railway was to take following more or less the line of the River Kwai. The earlier parties, who came up from Singapore, including my own, carried out this work. It entailed some arduous marches through very difficult terrain – virtually virgin jungle – accomplished by hacking one's way through with a *parang* and carrying such kit as one still possessed.

On arrival at the proposed campsite, the first job was to clear a sufficiently large area to house the camp. Thereafter, construction of the huts was started under the close supervision of Japanese engineers. Fortunately, it was not required of us to have any knowledge of hut construction in the same way that later parties required no knowledge of railway building. We only had to obey orders – we were the work forces.

In many ways the Japanese ignored the terms of the Geneva Convention laid down for the treatment of POWs. One of these was that Officers were not supposed to work. The Japanese got around this one by ordering the removal of all badges of rank, so there was no means of telling who were Officers and who were not. In any case, shirts were preserved to wear in the evenings, as a protection against mosquitoes during our years in the Thai jungle. It was, in any case, too hot and humid during the day to wear anything but a pair of shorts that became tattier and tattier as time passed. Latterly, most of us worked clad only in g-strings.

The huts in all these transit camps were of the standard *attap* construction already described in the camp at Bam Pong. There was no shortage of material for hut building, as the jungle consisted mainly of bamboo that gave nasty scratches on the legs as you foraged through it. These scratches usually turned into tropical ulcers and most POWs had one or more ulcers on their feet, ankles or calves. These would become quite deep, with a pocket of pus underneath and a scab on top. They never seemed to heal, and on occasion it was necessary to amputate the limb affected. I still have the scars from my ulcers on my feet and legs to this day. Fortunately, as we moved forward from Bam Pong, we were never very far from the river, where we were able to wash and swim in the evenings after work. I remember the cool water feeling marvellous on the ulcers, which were surrounded by an angry, red and very hot area of hard flesh. We also washed our clothes in the river and filled our water bottles from water collected upstream of the washing area, but only drank it after boiling.

The river was also used as a line of communication for Thai boats bringing up supplies, and it was possible surreptitiously to trade with the boat people out of sight of the Japanese guards. Many who still had watches sold them for Thai currency, which they would then spend sparingly on bananas, groundnuts or the occasional duck eggs. As the latter were very often bad, we soon learned never to buy eggs from the river boats without first immersing them in water to see if they floated or sank.

One had to be very careful carrying out transactions with the Thais since it meant a certain bashing if one was caught trading by one of the guards, possibly followed – depending on the mood of the guard – by a spell in the 'cooler'. This was rather like a sentry box for a midget in which you could neither stand up straight nor lie down. These 'coolers' got roasting hot by day, and very cold at night, and the majority of us tried to avoid doing anything to earn a visit to them.

However, there are always those of a more daring disposition than others, and there were always a few of this breed to be found in most of the camps up and down the railway. They became the black market racketeers and they were prepared to go out through the boundary fence of the camp at night and flog watches and other possessions to the Thais in the local *kampongs* for a commission, which they deducted from the price they paid to the vendor. These racketeers earned every penny of the commission they charged, as the risks they ran were considerable. Also, vitamin rich foodstuffs purchased with the money obtained in this way saved many a life. Sometimes the night runners brought back water bottles filled with rice wine, which they flogged in the camp by the half mug. Dark nights were a blessing for the racketeers, as every camp had armed sentries on duty in raised watch towers at each corner of the camp. These towers had a view of the whole boundary fence and any movement spotted near the perimeter by a guard brought forth a shout followed by a shot if the individual failed to show himself.

Certain of the larger camps had canteens where you could purchase food with local currency. This was alright as long as you had personal possessions with which to raise money, but after these ran out – as they invariably did – one could

often do a deal with a black marketeer in exchange for an IOU made out in the form of a cheque. The rate was Sing $1 = £1.

Life went on day after day with the perpetual hope of release within six months. Unfortunately, there was no variation in climate between spring, summer, autumn and winter, which would have helped to break the monotony. I have no recollection of celebrating Christmas, though we must have had three of these. Nor do I remember any birthdays. Nobody knew other people's birthday and we forgot our own. The climate was perpetually warm by day so our clothes, even as they became progressively more threadbare, were adequate. Nights were a different matter when one was reduced to a tatty pair of shorts and a khaki shirt. I managed to shave every day without soap and using the few blades I had preserved since captivity. Amongst our treasured possessions was the broken bottle for honing blades and the unbroken bottle for the 'toilet water'. A piece of burnt wood was a very necessary piece of equipment for cleaning teeth.

Parties to build the railway passed through our base camps on foot and eventually established themselves in the various camps which had been prepared up the length of the river. At one stage, the two forces selected to build the final stage of track through the worst part of the jungle, known as H and F Forces, passed through. These unfortunate groups would eventually link up the Siam side of the railway with that being built by POWs in Burma. We were not to see them again until about a year later at Chungkai – then we only saw about a third of the original lot – the only ones to survive and return.

Shortly after H and F Forces passed through, a serious cholera epidemic broke out and I believe all camps were affected to some extent. The combined outbreaks of cholera, malaria, dysentery and other ailments all took their toll of lives.

I have said little so far about Japanese torture, which was induced to a large extent by fear of reprisals from Tokyo if the railway schedule got behind. Basically, the High Command took it out on the Japanese officers in charge of our camps, who in turn took it out on our Korean guards, who in turn took it out on us.

As I mentioned before, the railway took a year to build, and throughout that year we listened to the incessant command of "Speedo, Speedo!" Those who failed to 'speedo' sufficiently for the guards' liking, either got beaten up or were made to stand in the sun holding a rock above their head. This was a favourite torture as a deviation from the 'cooler'. A lot of slow work was simply due to the fact that the individual was physically incapable of going any faster. This was particularly true on one occasion I remember when, because the railway was getting behind schedule, the Japanese ordered all hospital patients who could walk to join the work party. Some of these men, emaciated by dysentery or crippled by leg ulcers, simply could not endure an eight-hour day working in the sun, and many collapsed.

There were, however, also intentional go-slow tactics, such as the urgent call of "Speedo benjo!" which requested permission from the guard to stop work and retreat hastily to the nearest bush to avoid an accident. With so much dysentery around, the Japanese never quite knew how many of these calls were in fact genuine. All POWs realised the importance of retarding, as far as it was in their power, the completion of the vital supply link that would enable the Japanese to take the war closer to India. This aim was assisted in no small measure by the raids of US and RAF planes, which demolished bridges that had been constructed over ravines etc, shortly after they had been completed. I remember watching a raid on Tamarkan Bridge from a camp some two miles away at Kanchanaburi, known also as Kanburi.

One morning, I think towards the end of 1944, four British planes dive-bombed the bridge. The planes circled round and round, coming in low over the bridge and dropping their bombs. Every time a direct hit was made, a great cheer rose from the audience, although they knew that as soon as the raid was over, they would have to start rebuilding the bridge. This, I understand, was the bridge on the River Kwai referred to in the film of that name.

During 1943 and 1944 one of the main boosts to our spirits was a constant supply of news. Whereas in the early days we had to rely on bore-holes, it turned out that most of the camps up and down the line had acquired and hidden a radio somewhere. These radios were constructed and operated by very brave men – often signallers. When moving from camp to camp, the radio was dismantled, and the various parts concealed amongst the kit or clothing of the operators. The Japanese guards were constantly on the lookout for radios, knowing that they nullified the propaganda they fed us every day, and huts were often searched.

Only in one camp that I know of, did the Japanese discover a radio and the three individuals responsible for it. The whole camp was ordered to assemble on the square, where we were forced to watch a firing squad shoot down the culprits. Afterwards, a party was detailed off to dig graves on the camp perimeter and bury the bodies. The Commandant, who stood on a box in the middle of the square, then gave us a pep talk. He warned us that this was what would happen to anybody caught operating a radio in the future.

Within a short space of time, another radio magically appeared in the camp to be operated by three other brave men who, I am happy to say, were never caught. Needless to say, we never enquired too closely about how the various radio parts were obtained, though I imagine through night forages outside the fence to the local village. We all felt that the less we knew about where the radio was concealed in the camp, or how the various parts were transported on the move, the better. Knowing nothing would ensure that no amount of torture could force a man to reveal anything.

It was rumoured that certain parts, like the condensers, were buried in the tins of cooked rice, which made up our haversack rations, and batteries were concealed in the hollow bamboo poles carried on the shoulders of two men on which our possessions were slung when on the move. We must have moved camp many times during our three years in Thailand, and as we were always searched before leaving and on arrival at the new camp, it is surprising that the radios survived undetected.

The times of the news bulletins were known, and one member of the team of three would listen through the earpiece, while the other two took up a lounging position, one at each end of the hut. The two loungers were much more alert than they appeared to be to the casual observer, and were prepared to give an agreed signal at a moment's notice should a guard appear heading in the direction of the hut. The news was passed on verbally to one member of each hut throughout the camp. These hut reps would pass on the news to the two men sleeping at one end of the slats after lights out. It was then passed on from man to man down the hut until it reached the men at the other end.

After the railway building programme had been going for about six months, I went down with diphtheria and was sent back to the hospital camp at Chungkai where I found I was not the only sufferer from this disease. I met up again with Drummond-Black – Blackie, of our chummery in Bombay. It was the first time I had seen him since the OCTU in Belgaum.

Poor Blackie was in a bad way, but he never complained. He was on the slats next to me in the hospital hut. He died one night while I was asleep – he was there when I dropped off, but when I woke in the morning there was an empty space on the slats next to me.

There were quite a few men in the process of recovering from diphtheria when I was admitted, which was fortunate for me as a source of serum. The Japanese, true to form, provided no serum to the hospital, so our doctors were forced to use human serum. Being much less potent, however, about ten times the volume is required. Every patient who recovered from diphtheria gave a pint of blood, from which the serum was drawn off in a large syringe about one inch in diameter by six inches long, and this was pumped into new arrivals such as myself.

It didn't take long for the infection, which was in my nose, to clear up, but I then started to develop polyneuritis – a paralysis that starts at the extremities, in the toes and fingers. It creeps up until the whole of the arms and legs are

paralysed. The turning point came for me when I started to experience a vagus palsy, caused by paralysis of the vagus nerve, which controls the heartbeat. The effect was a substantial increase in the pulse rate and extreme difficulty in breathing. At this stage, the doctors decided to give an injection of their very limited supply of morphine, and immediately my breathing became easier. From then onwards, there was a steady improvement in my condition, and the feeling started to come back to my toes and fingers, working its way up the limbs. A test of the return of sensitivity was done each day by pricking the arms and legs with a needle, starting from the extremities and working progressively up the limbs. The point at which the needle could no longer be felt was recorded.

Altogether, I was horizontal for six months, during which time I had to perform daily exercises trying to lift one leg and then the other vertically off the bed, and similarly with the arms. After I could raise the limbs about a foot, I was propped with my legs over the side of the slats in a sitting position and had to spend half an hour each day trying to raise myself from the sitting to the standing position. The first time my legs were put over the side of the bed, they swung uncontrolled and uncontrollable like pendulums, till the doctor placed the feet on the floor.

When I talk about beds, these were, of course, bamboo slats as in all the other huts. The dedication of the doctors, working in the most primitive conditions, with the bare minimum of surgical instruments and drugs, had to be seen to be believed. The stench from the hospital hut was appalling and could be smelt even as you approached the hut from the outside. Many of the patients could not control their bowels as a result of dysentery, and most of them had suppurating ulcers that had to be regularly dressed. One man two places away from me down the slats developed uremia, and the urine exuded from his pores until one morning he got merciful release and died.

After the six months had elapsed, I was able to move around for short distances on crutches and talk to bedridden friends and patients in the hut. Many of them were in a sad state and were a shock to behold. Skeletons, with no flesh on their bones, where every bone in the rib-cage could be identified, and with arms and legs like spindles, yet mostly in their twenties. The daily burial rate at that time averaged fifteen. Yet, as I have said, it was fantastic what the doctors such as Duncan Black and the Australian Colonel Dunlop, nicknamed Weary, to mention just two, managed to do with little or no drugs at their disposal, most of them working for twelve hours or more each day.

After the railway construction had been completed, what remained of H and F Forces were brought back to Chungkai, and this laid a further burden on the doctors as these survivors of the worst rigours of the jungle were in a desperate state.

I have to look on the six months I spent in Chungkai hospital hut, and the following four months it took for me to learn to walk again, as a blessing in disguise, as I missed out on the worst period on the railway when the most lives were lost. I heard that in the northern jungle, where H and F Forces were working, many a man collapsed and died on the job and a detail of a few of his mates would be ordered to stop work and bury him. In addition to the large cemetery at Chungkai, with its little crosses still well kept, I am told, there lie hundreds of men in shallow graves close to the railway line – unmarked, now overgrown and part of the Thai jungle.

Altogether in the year it took to construct the railway, we lost a life for every sleeper that was laid. Those of H and F Forces who made it back to Chungkai, apart from being debilitated from dysentery and malaria, had massive ulcers on their insteps and calves. Many of these were so deep that the pus had to be removed daily with a sterilised spoon. This had to be done without any form of anaesthetic and caused some of the men to pass out with the pain. This was a blessing, as the subsequent dousing of the wound with Dettol would have been even harder to bear if they had been conscious.

Apart from a relatively modest loss of weight (I was not a heavy man to start with), my condition at this time was not bad. I was able to hobble around the camp on my crutches and the only pain I experienced was from the ulcers on my legs which, as an effect of diphtheria, had become covered with a hard jet black crust which could not be removed. The swollen red area around the ulcers became very painful when the legs were vertical and the blood was surging to these areas. Eventually, as the diphtheria eliminated itself from the system, the crusts dropped off and the ulcers were then cleaned of pus and treated with disinfectant and sulphur powder.

By this time we had learnt from the news bulletins that the tide was beginning to turn against the Japanese, and that the war was also going well for us in Europe. This raised our spirits, and my memory is of enjoying quite a happy few months in Chungkai while recuperating. Good books were passed around, as many of us still had a book amongst our belongings. We also had lectures in the evenings on every conceivable subject. The Dutch contingent had started preparing culinary delicacies called *sambal* in three varieties, egg, peanut, and what was known as dynamite – made from raw chillies. They also produced a sweet delicacy called peanut stars. A kind of canteen had been set up in the camp and the Dutch used to flog these goodies to those who could afford them. A small portion of *sambal* certainly helped to get down the perpetual boiled rice of our daily diet. Bridge and chess were played for small stakes amongst the real gamblers, as on the result would depend whether you could pay a visit to the canteen or not.

There was by now a lot of movement on the railway line coming from the direction of Burma. Whereas previously we had seen regular truckloads of troops going north, there now seemed to be a preponderance of trucks coming south carrying wounded Japanese troops back to base hospitals in Malaya. Every one of these truckloads raised our spirits a little higher.

One day a group of us was told that as we were now mobile we were to be transferred to another camp where there was some work. We were to have our first experience of travelling on our railway as we were bundled into trucks and taken south to Kanburi. This must have been around July or August 1944. I didn't stay long in Kanburi, and the only feature that stands out in my memory is watching the air raid on the Tamarkan Bridge already referred to. By that time there was quite a lot of aerial activity, and a plane flying very high apparently dropped a few thousand leaflets. One of these was found by one of our working parties on the roads. It said, "Hold on! We are coming."

I was moved from Kanburi to Nom Pladak, which was a camp situated at the head of the old railway line from Malaya and the start of the continuation of the line that we had built to the Burma border. The camp was situated close to the railway junction. My memory of the camp is vivid even now because of the air raid.

One morning, shortly after dawn, we heard the air-raid siren and the Japanese scurried from their observation towers into slit trenches. As we had nowhere to hide, those from the hospital hut – other than bed patients – stood on the central square and watched with fascinated eyes an arrowhead of bombers heading straight in our direction. We couldn't distinguish the markings on the planes, as they were flying too high, but the fact that the sirens had been sounded implied that they were of the Allies, and a great cheer went up from the assembled crowd.

Changi Aug. 31 1945
Ronald Searle

First Parachute Supplies dropping over Changi Gaol

Suddenly, the atmosphere of euphoria turned to panic as we saw a clutch of bombs being released from each plane and falling ever closer to where we were standing. In no time at all, everyone was lying flat on the ground and saying three Hail Marys or whatever. When the bombs landed, the noise was simply deafening, and as I looked up, I saw two things: the first was that the bombs had over-shot our camp by about 200 yards and had in fact hit their target which was the adjacent railway junction and yard. The second thing I saw was that there were six or seven other sorties of planes following the first, each sortie comprised of seven planes in arrowhead formation. At this point in time, as a betting man, I wouldn't have accepted an even money bet on my chance of survival.

The second sortie made a direct hit on our hospital hut, which was about 100 yards from where I lay, and there were still five more to come. I am sure we all suffered the same fear as we watched the bomb traps open under the planes and followed the bombs with our eyes as they hurtled down with an ever-increasing screech, but each time they went just over us and hit their target, the railway yard. There were forty-three prisoners killed as a result of the direct hit on the hospital hut, and the next morning we had a funeral service for them and a burial party to carry the makeshift coffins to a mass grave prepared by us the previous evening outside the camp. Every prisoner in the camp was there.

One day, probably towards the end of 1944 or early 1945, we were told to assemble on the parade ground where the Japanese Camp Commandant addressed us. He told us that all Officers who were fit to be moved were being transferred to an Officers' camp. All the fit Officers, including myself, were entrained in trucks and carried for what seemed like a long distance. Finally, the train stopped at a point in the middle of the jungle. It was night and pouring with rain. We were ordered to detrain and after being lined up and counted, were marched behind a guard who led the way on a most uncomfortable and tiring journey which eventually brought us to Nakom Nyok – the first Officers' camp.

After a night's sleep, we surveyed our new surroundings. The camp was a big one, to house Officers from all the camps up and down the railway who were being segregated from their troops for the first time. Indian Army Officers, like myself, hadn't of course seen our troops since capitulation day in 1942. The camp would be made up of British, Australian and Dutch. The camp was surrounded on all four sides by a very wide ditch with a barbed wire fence on the outside. Each corner had a tower housing a sentry behind a machine gun. The camp was in a clearing in the jungle and there was flat land on all four sides for several hundred yards. There was no doubt in our minds that morning, that when the drive from Burma under Mountbatten started, we were not to be allowed to escape. The positioning of the machine guns was very ominous.

Life at Nokom Nyok was much more relaxed than it had been since the days of Changi. The railway having been completed, the Japanese no longer adopted the "Speedo, Speedo" attitude, and although we still went out on working parties on such tasks as road works and brick making, these were leisurely by comparison. After the work parties returned to camp, evenings were spent playing bridge or attending talks. The news continued to get better and around the middle of 1945, I think, we all realised that we didn't have much longer to wait. The feeling of euphoria, however, was tempered by the uncertainty of what would happen to us if there was a landing of Allied troops on the beaches of Thailand or a drive through Burma. We couldn't envisage the Japanese leaving us behind if they found themselves with their backs to the wall.

One day in August 1945, we were out as usual on a road repair party. However, this day was different in that, around midday we were all ordered back to camp by our guard – normally this only happened at 6pm. As we marched back, we were joined by other working parties converging on us from other directions, and all heading back to camp. As we neared the camp perimeter, we were given the V sign from Thais on the roadside.

Could this really be the end? We were reluctant to raise our hopes too much as we had heard so many rumours in the past few months, all of which had proved to be unfounded. Logically, it didn't seem possible, as there hadn't even been an Allied landing in Malaya or Thailand. We understood the Japanese well enough by this time to know that they would not simply hand back all the territory they had acquired over the past years without a struggle. We had, of course, no knowledge of the Hiroshima or Nagasaki bombings.

Shortly after our return to the camp, the Japanese Commandant sent for Colonel Toosey, the Senior British Officer, and informed him of the capitulation. The administration of the camp was immediately handed over to the British and Allies, and the Japanese made themselves scarce by moving outside the perimeter of the camp beyond the barbed wire. They were obviously scared of reprisals, and I know there must have been many amongst us who would have dearly loved to pay back some old scores.

Under our administration, life at Nakom Nyok took on a new meaning. An atmosphere of euphoria prevailed, and we found it hard to believe that the war was over and that we were actually going home instead of being driven, as we had feared, ahead of a retreating Japanese army and in all likelihood being annihilated in the process. This is what the Hiroshima incident achieved, and while there are many in Britain and elsewhere who still think that the dropping of the bomb was wrong, not one of the thousands in the concentration camps in Thailand and Malaya at that moment in time would agree with them. The bomb, by bringing about the immediate capitulation of Japan, saved tens of thousands of POWs, and we felt it was a bit of poetic justice in that the Japanese had started the war with the bombing of Pearl Harbour. Our losses on the construction of the railway were estimated at 130,000 dead.

British and American planes were in evidence in the sky the next day, coming in low over the camp, and as we watched a great cheer went up. Things were being dropped from the planes – not bombs, but bundles with a parachute attached which opened and drifted down. The bundles contained tinned food, cigarettes and medicines – all the things we had been starved of during the past three and-a-half years. Of the Red Cross parcels that had been sent to us regularly under the Geneva Convention, we had only had one issue from the Japanese during the entire period. The rest had obviously been purloined for their own troops. We had to be patient for several days before we were released, and during this period we were under our own administration, and Colonel Toosey took over as Camp Commandant. The strictest discipline had to be maintained, which in retrospect can't have been easy.

It is difficult to convince men who have been interned for three and-a-half years that they must stay inside the confines of the camp perimeter when they know that the war is over. However, it was vital that, to avoid incidents, no contact should be made with the Japanese who were by now somewhere outside the camp.

In this, Colonel Toosey did a first class job.

CHAPTER TWELVE

HOMEWARD BOUND
AUGUST 1945 – SEPTEMBER 1945

At last, the long awaited day arrived when we were formed into groups and taken in trucks to Bangkok airport where we were assembled in a hangar. The groups were led on a rota system to the tarmac to board the Dakotas, and eventually it was my group that was at the head of the queue.

In a short time we were seated on the floor of the aircraft with our kit-bags containing all that remained of our possessions between our knees. Soon the engines were revving and we were speeding down the runway and airborne. Although the Dakota was carrying a heavier complement than it was designed for, this was the first time that I experienced no nerves at all on take off as to whether the plane would make it or not. We had come through and we were free!

After landing at Rangoon, we were taken to hospitals where we went through a medical examination. I then arranged for a message to be sent to my mother, informing her that I was safe and well. Those of us who were not confined to bed were now free to go on the town, which is exactly what we did. The hospitality of the people of Rangoon at that time was quite unbelievable. After being issued with a new tropical kit – including an Australian bush hat – I joined a group at the hospital entrance where a procession of cars rolled up throughout that evening.

The cars belonged to British civilians or services, and each car took a few of us. The procedure was that the car driver would announce the number he could take and those at the front of the queue piled in. We didn't know where we were going, and we couldn't have cared less. As it turned out, the parties that had been laid on for us by both civilians and services were magnificent. Some of us ended up in military messes for a dinner dance, and some in the houses of our hosts, where dinner and dancing were also laid on.

The effect of the transition from our previous lifestyle to this one in such a short space of time is difficult to describe. One anomaly that we all experienced, was the difficulty in understanding the female voice. Not having heard one for years, the high pitched tones tended to jar on our ears, and we had to listen very carefully in order to conduct a sensible conversation. We had to go very carefully with alcohol, which went straight to our heads after even just a couple of drinks. During the entire period of our stay in Rangoon, the cars rolled up at the hospital entrance at 7pm every evening like clockwork. One night I was taken, with a couple of others, to an Air Force mess where a dance was in progress. Shortly after arrival, I was dragged on to the dance floor to join in the Hokey Cokey – evidently the latest craze – the object being to snake in file round the room, weaving in and out of tables holding on to the waist of the person in front of you. During this ritual which resembled a tribal dance, everybody stopped at prescribed intervals to shake their left leg, their right leg, their left arm, their right arm and finally their whole self. It was easily learned, very noisy and good fun.

At a time when everybody was enjoying himself to the full, it is sad to relate two tragic incidents that occurred while we were in Rangoon. One chap died as a result of eating a whole tin of bully beef (corned beef). His stomach had been starved of meat protein for so long on a rice diet, that it was unable to cope with such a large quantity. Another chap, after enduring and surviving three and-a-half years of hell, shot himself on learning that his wife, assuming him to be dead, had re-married.

We had a visit from Earl Mountbatten who went round all the hospitals visiting the sick in the wards. Afterwards, those of us who were mobile were assembled in the quadrangle where he mounted a rostrum and made a memorable speech welcoming us back.

After enjoying the entertainment laid on for us by the people of Rangoon for about a week, I was pronounced fit to go home and joined a group to be flown to Calcutta. On arrival there, we found that the whole of the foyer of the Great Eastern Hotel had been taken over by the Repatriation of Allied Prisoners of War India (RAPWI) Organisation. There were counters for documentation, issue of back pay for the period we had been interned, and issue of air, rail or sea tickets to take us home.

I had decided that I should call on my office in Bombay to see if they still knew of my existence, so after spending a day or two in Calcutta completing formalities, I caught a plane to Bombay. I found the office much as I had left it, if rather depleted in managerial staff, and got a great welcome from everyone including the Indian clerical staff. I learnt to my great sadness that, of my close friends, John Milligan had been killed in the Western Desert campaign and Gilby had died of wounds when fighting with Wingate's Chindits in Burma. My manager told me that I could have six months leave in England on full pay.

I sailed from Bombay on the *Mauretania* towards the middle of September 1945. This was the last ship to carry POWs home from the Far East and there were only a handful of us on board – perhaps forty or fifty. The ship was filled with troops going home on repatriation made up of British Army units and girls from the Women's Services. Conditions on board were fairly crowded, even for a liner the size of the *Mauretania*.

I had become friendly with one of the WAAF officers, a girl called Diana Orlebar, who turned out to be the daughter of the famous Battle of Britain pilot of that name. We were looking forward to going ashore together at the various ports of call, and by the time we reached Suez, I, particularly, was getting bored with being cooped up in an overcrowded ship, and a bit claustrophobic.

Imagine our feelings when it was announced that none of the passengers was to be allowed ashore. Evidently all the ships that had sailed from Bombay during the preceding weeks had allowed all their passengers ashore, as those ships had only POWs as passengers, and it was convenient to allow them ashore at Suez for fitting out with winter service kit. In the case of the *Mauretania*, however, with its mere handful of ex-POWs, it was much simpler from an administrative point of view to send the warm clothing on board by launch, and this is exactly what happened.

We had dropped anchor about a mile from shore when, around 6pm, as a group of us was standing at the rail, we saw a launch approaching carrying a party of a dozen or so Red Cross officials, male and female. I think it was then that the possibility occurred to me of getting ashore surreptitiously in the Red Cross launch when it eventually returned. Having made enquiries about the departure time of the *Mauretania*, it appeared that the ship was taking oil and water on board and was scheduled to sail from Suez at 2am. This then was the deadline for return to the ship, as I had no wish to be left behind in Suez, literally, without a paddle and little money.

I discussed my plan with Diana who was a girl game for anything involving a bit of excitement, and in this respect took after her father. It took the Red Cross about two hours to issue us with kit that fitted, and at about 8pm they started to wend their way into the bowels of the ship to rejoin their launch from F Deck. Diana and I managed to push our way into the middle of the group as they went down the gangway, and in the darkness boarded the launch unnoticed. About halfway to the shore somebody realised that the launch had two additional passengers and we had to admit that we were in fact passengers from the *Mauretania*.

Fortunately, the Red Cross was sympathetic and agreed to help us as far as they could. They suggested dropping us off at a point between Suez and Port Tewfik, because they assured us we would be caught if we went ashore with them at Suez.

We were dropped off on a lonely bit of coastline and, after wishing us good luck, they left us to our own devices as the launch turned around and headed for Suez. We found a road that ran close to and parallel with the shore, turned right on to this and after a short walk arrived at Port Tewfik.

There was not much there apart from some oil installations and an army barracks. The only sign of life came from a building that turned out to be the Sergeants' Mess. Having removed our badges of rank to avoid looking conspicuous, we entered the Mess, which was quite crowded, and elbowed our way to the bar. Our plan was to stay on till around midnight and then hire a local craft to ferry us back to the ship. We had to hope, of course, that the gangways would still be down and that we could sneak on board unobserved. We got into a happy group at the bar that saw nothing odd about our being from the *Mauretania*, as passengers from all the previous ships had been free to come ashore.

Unfortunately for us, our group of Sergeants was joined at about 11pm by two pilots from the Harbour Board to whom we were introduced as troops from the *Mauretania*.

The fat was really in the fire then, as the pilots turned to us and said, "But no passengers from the 'Mauretania' are allowed ashore..."

This was a difficult situation to bluff our way out of, and we had to come clean, not knowing whether the officials would decide to hand us over to the authorities. Fortunately, having imbibed a few beers, they were quite sympathetic, while warning us that we would be in serious trouble if we were found out in our little escapade. The pilots had to go out to clear the ship for passage through the Suez Canal, and Diana, by making the most of her feminine charms, persuaded them to take us out surreptitiously in their launch under cover of darkness and offload us at the companionway.

At about midnight we left the Mess and walked to the Pilot Boat that was moored in Port Tewfik harbour. The weather had deteriorated in the past few hours, and the sea was quite rough with a strong breeze blowing. When we had covered the mile or so to the ship, we found that she had swung round on her anchor, with the result that the companionway from which we had disembarked was now on the windward side of the ship facing away from the land. The pilots said it would be too risky to take their small launch alongside on the windward side, as the sea was too rough. We therefore had to heave to on the leeward, or shore, side where there were already an oil tanker and a water ship alongside, making it impossible to board without crossing one of these two vessels.

The Pilot Boat drew up alongside the tanker and we stepped onto it after thanking the pilots for their help. We ran across the deck of the tanker and saw there was an open hatch on F Deck of the *Mauretania* about three feet below the level of the tanker deck. Unfortunately, there was a gap of about six feet between the two vessels caused by the oil pipe joining them. There was nothing below the gap but water. There was nothing for it – we had to jump!

We positioned ourselves opposite the open hatch and Diana climbed over the tanker rail. On a count of three, I gave her a great push with the maximum strength I could muster and, thank God, she landed on all fours inside the hatch. I followed by pushing myself off the rails and also landed on all fours. We ran through F Deck and the galleys and eventually found our way to our cabins without meeting a soul. To this day nobody knows that two of the passengers on the *Mauretania* went ashore in Port Tewfik in September 1945!

As it happened, we were unable to sail as scheduled as the Pilots refused to clear the ship for passage through the Suez Canal on account of the strong crosswinds. The *Mauretania* was by far the largest liner ever to pass through the Canal, and the Pilots decided it would be unsafe in prevailing conditions, in view of the small clearance between the ship and the banks of the Canal. The Captain was reported to be furious as he was trying to break the record for the run from Bombay to Liverpool. We were held at Suez for another twenty-four hours, but the Captain, not to be outdone, claimed the record on arrival at Liverpool on the basis of eleven days sailing time although the actual time taken was twelve days.

The rain was pouring down in Liverpool docks as the large liner, with hooters blowing, was towed to her berth. However, this didn't deter a brass band from playing a welcome for us on the quayside, and quite a large crowd assembled in a long line, cheering loudly.

After disembarking, we were conducted to a shed where we went through a process of filling up endless forms – we were back amidst the red tape – typical service-style bureaucracy which took the best part of two hours to complete.

After that was finished, we were issued with civilian kit and I was able to telephone home. Eventually we were told that the formalities were finally over and that to ensure that we enjoyed our first evening home, many of the local girls were waiting for us in a nearby hall, where a dance band was in attendance and was prepared to go on playing until the last couple left the floor. I remember I met a girl, but can't remember her name for the life of me. What I do remember was that I rather rashly offered to walk her home, and then found that she lived in Magull, a suburb a long way out of the docks to which, having dropped her, I had to plod wearily back as dawn was breaking.

The next thing I can remember is travelling by train through England and Scotland, heading for Glasgow. It was now the end of September, and from the train window the landscape looked beautiful to me. I had left Liverpool in autumn 1938, and seven eventful years had elapsed since I said goodbye to my mother and my friends at home.

I had made many new friends and, sadly, some of the best of them had been killed. I had seen death and destruction on a horrendous scale. I had had moments of appalling fear. I had witnessed cruelty, torture, deprivation and sickness beyond anything I could have imagined. I had seen the worst in men and the best in men: the incredible fortitude, the indomitable strength of the human spirit in adversity. The inhumanity and degradation that we prisoners had suffered would be hard to describe to anyone. But in all that awfulness, I had come across many instances of the solidarity and loyalty, of the steadfastness and unbelievable bravery that could exist among such a disparate gathering of men. I had left England as a carefree, inexperienced youth, and I was returning as a mature man.

As the train chugged its way through the autumn countryside, I knew it would be incredibly difficult to convey these feelings or describe my experiences in any relevant way to my mother and her genteel sisters. I reflected on how much I had changed, how much I had learned about myself.

I realised that one thought above all had kept me going. Some of the best years of my life had been spent in conditions of dreadful hardship, so I was determined to survive in order to spend my remaining years enjoying life and having fun!

EPILOGUE

The battle's o'er, the unrelenting toil,
And all for what, to those
Who prematurely found their last repose
In alien soil.

MESSAGE FROM H.E. THE C-IN-C

"I WISH I COULD GREET YOU PERSONALLY ON YOUR RETURN TO INDIA. YOUR GREAT COURAGE AND FORTITUDE DURING CAPTIVITY IN THE HANDS OF A BARBARIC AND RUTHLESS ENEMY HAS BEEN THE ADMIRATION OF US ALL. I WISH YOU A SPEEDY RETURN TO YOUR FAMILIES AND HOPE THAT YOU WILL ENJOY A WELL EARNED AND LONG AWAITED REST GOOD LUCK TO YOU ALL."

ہزایکسیلنسی کمانڈرانچیف کا پیغام

میری دلی تمنا تو یہ تھی کہ آپ لوگوں کے ہندوستان واپس آنے پر میں خود ہی مبارکباد دیتا، تاہم ایک ظالم اور بے رحم دشمن کی قید میں آپ لوگوں نے جس صبر و ضبط، ثابت قدمی اور استقلال کا ثبوت دیا وہ یقیناً قابل تعریف ہے۔

میں چاہتا ہوں کہ اب آپ لوگ جلدی ہی اپنے عزیزوں دل سے جا ملیں اور مدّت کے بعد اُس آرام سے لطف اندوز ہوں جس کے آپ مستحق ہیں۔

میری دُعائیں آپ کے ساتھ ہیں۔"

प्रधान सेनापति का संदेश

मेरी इच्छा थी कि आप के भारत में पहुंचने के अवसर पर मैं स्वय उपस्थित होता और आपको अभि वादन करता। बर्बर और निर्मम शत्रु के हाथों में बन्दी रहने की स्थिति में आपने जिस साहस और धैर्य का परिचय दिया है, उसकी हम सभी प्रशंसा करते हैं

"मेरी कामना है कि आप शीघ्र अपने परिवारों के पास पहुंचें और सुदीर्घ अवधि तक आराम करें, जिसके आप पात्र हैं और जिसकी प्रतीक्षा में आप बहुत दिनों से रहे हैं।

सबका मंगल हो "

The Following is a Personal Message from Their Majesties The King and Queen To Repatriated Prisoners of War

The Queen and I bid you a very warm welcome home.

Through all the great trials & sufferings which you have undergone at the hands of Japanese you and your comrades have been constantly in our thoughts. We know from the accounts we have already received how heavy those sufferings have been. We know also that these have been endured by you with the highest courage.

We mourn with you the deaths of so many of your gallant comrades.

With all our hearts we hope that your return from captivity will bring you and your families a full measure of happiness which you may long enjoy together.

George R.I.

BL [stamp] No 65 A

M.I. 9/JAP/ N° 111819 A

NIL

WRITE IN BLOCK CAPITAL LETTERS IN PENCIL

No. Ec 297   Rank Captain   Surname KENDALL

Christian Names Peter Gordon   Decorations —

Ship (R.N., R.A.N. or Merchant Navy) ....   Unit & Div. (Army) 2/17 Dogra Regt.

Squadron and Command (R.A.F., R.A.A.F., etc.) ....

Date of Birth 17.4.16   Date of Enlistment 26.1.40.

Private Address and Telephone No. 17 Crown Terrace, Glasgow. W.2. Scotland

Place and Date of Original Capture Singapore. 15.2.42
(Aircrew R.A.F. to give place and date of a/c crash).

1. What camps, detachments or hospitals were you in ? Give dates and names of the British Camp Leaders, Detachment. (or Block) Leaders or, in the case of hospitals, the Senior British Medical Officers.

Camp or Hospital.	Dates.	Camp Leader.	Detachment or Block Leader (if any).
Bampong (Thailand)	1.11.42 to 7.11.42	Lt. Col Swinton (E. Surreys)	
Chunkai ,,	20.12.42 to 30.6.43	Lt. Col Outram (137 Fd Regt R.A.)	
Wan Rang ,,	10.11.42 to 17.12.42	Lt. Col Swinton (E. Surreys)	
Nong Pladuk ,,	5.10.43 to 22.1.45	Lt. Col Toosey (135 Fd Regt R.A.)	
Kandianburi	26.1.45 to 15.6.45	2.7.43 to 30.9.43 } Lt. Col McEachern (Australia)	
Nakom Nyok ,,	24.6.45 to 30.6.45	Lt. Col Toosey (135 Fd Regt R.A.)	

2. ESCAPES OR ATTEMPTED ESCAPES. (Additional paper will be supplied on request if required).

(a) Give full description and approx. date of each attempt you made to escape, showing how you left the camp, and from which camp each attempt was made. State whether there was an air-raid in progress at the time or not. If an escape was made from a train or vehicle the approx. speed and how it was guarded should be included.

(b) Were you physically fit when you made these attempts ?

(c) Give Regimental particulars of anyone who accompanied you on each attempt.

What happened to them ?

(d) Give briefly your experiences during periods of freedom.

(e) How were you recaptured and on what date ?

110

(f) Do you know of any attempts made by other people to escape ? Give their Regimental particulars and full description of their experiences.

3. ESCAPE COMMITTEES. GIVE NAMES OF ANY INDIVIDUAL P/W KNOWN TO YOU WHO WERE ORGANISERS OF ESCAPE AND RESISTANCE GENERALLY.

(a)

Name.	Regiment or Corps., Sqn., etc.	Location	Date.

(b) DO YOU KNOW ANYTHING OF THEIR PLANS ?

4. SABOTAGE. DID YOU DO ANY SABOTAGE OR DESTRUCTION OF ENEMY FACTORY PLANT, WAR MATERIAL, COMMUNICATIONS, ETC., WHILE EMPLOYED IN WORKING PARTIES OR DURING ESCAPE ? (GIVE DETAILS, PLACES AND NAMES).

5. DID YOU OBSERVE ANY COURAGEOUS ACTS PERFORMED BY ALLIED PERSONNEL ? (GIVE NAMES, PLACES, ETC.)

A Wireless Set was run by the Webber Brothers (Argyll and Sutherland Highlanders) from Jan 1945 till August 1945. These brothers knew that at a neighbouring camp 3 officers had been discovered running a set and had been beaten to death. In spite of this they continued to give us news bulletins. I think both brothers were Lieutenant

6. Have you any other matter of any kind which you wish to bring to notice ?

111

POSTSCRIPT

My dear mother had always been assiduous in writing to me regularly, keeping me in touch with what was going on back home. Her letters were a great comfort to me, as I am sure mine were to her. But during my period in Malaya many of the letters she wrote never reached me.

The letters that are transcribed on the following pages were returned to my mother, often after many months, and I can only imagine the distress she must have felt on receiving them back.

What a cruel time the last three and-a-half years of the war must have been for her, not knowing whether I was alive or dead, but always optimistic for my eventual return, which might not have come to pass but for the atomic bomb.

The only communication she had received from me during the entire period was from Changi shortly after the fall of Singapore. It was a printed card which the Japanese had permitted us to sign, and which read simply:

I AM WELL.
I AM BEING WELL TREATED.

To: Capt P G Kendall
c/o Hong Kong & Shanghai Bank
Sungei Patani
Kedah
Malaya

Arashiyama
Grantown-on-Spey
Morayshire

3rd October 1941

My darling Peter,

What an address! I shall have to print it on the envelope.

*Well I was glad to get two letters since I wrote you last. One dated
1st Aug arrived five days before the one dated 8th July! Mails are
very peculiar. I note you got three of mine in one day. Some of yours
have taken four months en route, but this 1st Aug one has come in
less than two months.*

*I am afraid you will find your present quarters very quiet after
Singapore, but I hope dear that you didn't mean literally that the
inactivity is "getting you down". I worried a bit about that as that is
the very worst thing that can happen in the Army in such a climate
as you are now in.*

*It's such an awful climate at any time, but if one allows it to
get one down – it's fatal, and one has to keep oneself bright and
active, and as you know a Captain is a great incentive to his men.
Actually, I am thankful the fighting has not reached your part
of the world, but I think I'd rather have it there than you should
become lethargic and depressed through boredom and inaction.
That is the horror of war and is why the forces here have to be kept
entertained with sport, wireless programmes, concerts, dances, etc.
as it is bad for them even in this country, and what it must be like
where you are must be awful. Anyhow dear, I know you know it is
essential to keep yourself bright and fit and not allow yourself to
become morbid – no matter how hard the conditions. It would be
so utterly unlike you. Anyhow, knowing you, I would be foolish to
worry about it, as probably all you meant was that you were merely
"fed up" at being so long in getting your chance of smashing the
Jerries! Have patience, it will come.*

*Have just finished tea and on re-reading your letter I don't think
I need have written the foregoing, as you seem to be having a very
good time socially, which I am very glad to hear. I am glad Bobby
Longwill* (Editor's note: PGK's best school friend) *is in the same place.
Mrs Burns doesn't know where John* (Editor's note: later Sir John
Burns, MD Finlay's, Bombay office) *is stationed, so just continues to
write c/o Finlays Bombay as she has always done. Seems to me such
a roundabout way. I called to see her when I was home and she is
very anxious to know what John's wife is doing out there when her
people are in Sussex, so evidently John hasn't given her much news.*

*I am glad you enjoyed your party at Alor Star, and you were
lucky, as usual, at the races. Speaking of golf, I met Theo* (Editor's

note: a school friend of PGK*) in Hyndland the morning I was leaving. He had just come home on leave for a few days, and was just on his way to see me as his mother had told him I was at home. However, I was able to talk to him for a few minutes. He has got very much fatter but looking well. He said he had had a letter from you, but as you didn't mention any of the news in his previous letter, he wondered if you had received it. He said he would visit you when he got back to camp. Sandy Johnstone (*Editor's note: Alexander Vallance Ridley Johnstone, PGK's class mate and friend, of 602 City of Glasgow Squadron, later Air Vice Marshall) has been sent overseas but of course I don't know where. I said it might be Singapore, but his mother said it was somewhere where the fighting is going on she thought.*

I am most interested in your special job but of course you can't tell me anything about it as you say. Anyhow it will make things more interesting for you getting about the country a bit. What would Theo not give to be in your shoes. He is very fed up as life is very monotonous here he says, but it has been perfect peace since the Russians came in. We have a lot to thank them for.

*I arrived back here beginning of this month and we have plenty to do with Red Cross and canteen work. Het enjoyed Pitlochry but likes Grantown better and is glad to be back. Very delightful people staying here. Suits Het (*Editor's note: a friend of PGK's mother) as she is very particular whom she mixes with. A bit snobby on that point!*
*Nessie Forbes was married this week in Perth to a guardsman. It was a military wedding and she is in the WAAF's. Billie, (*Editor's note: PGK's mother's boyfriend, brother of John Burns), Helen and John went through for the wedding, also Alastair if he could get leave. He is in the Air Force.*

Well dear, no more news, so will get off to post. Weather still lovely.

All my love,
Your loving
Mother

Editor's note: This letter was marked OPENED BY CENSOR and returned to PGK's mother in May 1942 stamped IT IS REGRETTED THIS ITEM COULD NOT BE DELIVERED AT THE ADDRESS STATED.

To: Capt P G Kendall
1/17th Dogra Regiment
c/o Hong Kong & Shanghai Bank
Sungei Patani
Kedah
Malaya

Arashiyama
Grantown-on-Spey
Morayshire

20th October 1941

No. 93

My darling Peter

I have very little news this letter as each day is more or less like the
last with Red Cross, canteen and collecting, but I am enjoying it
thoroughly. There is a lot to be done, but it is all very interesting, and
the people very delightful. Miss McGregor (daughter of the owner of
this house) is Vice President of the Red Cross.

There are four of us staying here and we are most comfortable.
Good fires and food and a most lovely house. One of the ladies said
yesterday that we are living in the lap of luxury in wartime, but we
are all doing our bit to help, which is all we can do. I am feeling
particularly well and enjoying the interest of it all. Mrs Grant said
when I was home last month I had lost 10 years off my age! One
lady staying here is the double of Mrs Thomson (Sheila's mother) in
looks and manner and speech. A marvellous likeness!

I have just had a letter from Nan (Editor's note: Nettie's eldest
sister, PGK's aunt) telling us Ethel McCombie is engaged to a
Norwegian. She has only known him for 2 months but they have
been seeing each other every day. I met him when I was home and
he is a very plain looking little man, but I should think has a lovely
nature – which Ethel says is the case. He speaks English, but not
at all fluently, rather brokenly. Before she met him she was very
friendly with another Norwegian, and very keen on him. He was very
handsome. Tall and not unlike the Duke of Kent, and I could have
understood it had it been him. He has been away on his ship for 4
months but arrived back on leave in Sept and called when the other
man was there. Evidently great antagonism between the two men
and the one wanted to know what the other was to her, etc, etc, and
she was at her wits' end. However, the tall one (who was 12 years
younger than her incidentally) went off next day to rejoin his ship

and now she is engaged to the other one. I hope she realises what she is doing as if she marries him she will have to take Norwegian nationality and live in Norway after the war. She hasn't told us about it yet, but I had a pc this am saying she would be visiting us with some news after Inglebert sails on Wednesday, so no doubt I'll be hearing the details then. He has to be away for six months, so time may help her to weigh up the pros and cons. The Norwegians are a nice race, but at her age I think she will not easily take to new conditions and mode of life.

I think I told you in my last letter Sandy has been sent overseas, also that I met Theo when I was home and he was wondering if you had got his letter as you never mentioned any of its news in yours to him.

I am looking forward to having another letter from you, but goodness knows when that will be as I had two within a week which I answered in my last to you. Your letters are very interesting, dear, and I am truly thankful you are keeping so well.

Well I am due at the canteen in 15 minutes so must get off. The lads here are all very nice – all British troops – and we cater well for them.
All my love dear,
Your loving
Mother

Editor's note: This letter was marked OPENED BY CENSOR and returned to PGK's mother stamped NO SERVICE – RETURN TO SENDER on 2nd May 1942.

To: Capt P G Kendall
1/17th Dogra Regiment
c/o Hong Kong & Shanghai Bank
Sungei Patani
Kedah
Malaya

Arashiyama
Grantown-on-Spey
Morayshire

3rd November 1941

No. 94

My darling Peter

I was so glad to get your letter of 19th August yesterday. Miss Fraser
of Craiglyme phoned to tell me it was there, and I went round and
collected it.

How terrible about poor Gibby. I'm sure it must have been a
terrible shock to you. It's ghastly to think of all those fine young lads
being taken away. I just can't bear to think what it must mean to his
poor mother. It was very thoughtful of you to write to her, dear. I'm
so glad you did, and Gibby would have been pleased had he known.
I'm quite sure he does, in a better world than this. Nice of you to
give up the Penang outing, but of course I knew you would do that in
the sad circumstances. I know you will feel very upset with so many
of your Belgaum friends being killed, but Egypt has been a bad sport,
and I have always been truly thankful that you were not sent there.
As you say, it seems like fate.

I am enclosing some cuttings with this letter. One of Mabel
Gilmour's wedding. I don't know the man, but you may. The other
is an article about Sandy's battalion. I told you he had been sent
overseas, but it must be with a different squadron, as I see the new
squadron leader is a New Zealander. I also enclose a bit of Lord
Provost Nolan's article on his retirement (he did so on Saturday) in
which he mentions the 602 Glasgow Squadron, with the names of
the fighter pilots. I notice Archie McKellar is one of them, but don't
know if he is in the photos as I didn't know him. You may recognise
some of them.

I'm glad you have made a bit on your investments. I knew you'd
look after it. Yes, Father told me he had cabled you, also. The others
wrote to you. Hope you received their letters. Billie Burns, F. Munro,
E. McCombie, Bella McC, McWilliams, Mrs Grant, etc, whom I

saw when home, all asked me to send congratulations. B. Burns
said "How does it feel to be the mother of a Captain?" I said "Very
proud!" and I certainly am. You've fulfilled all my hopes for you, in
every way.

Don't worry about my going out alone at night. Wild horses
wouldn't drag me. One experience like that was quite enough,
and I was dashed lucky in that. We never go out after dinner,
unless to pictures, and then only if McGregors are going, when we
go in their car.

Well no more this time, dear, as letter will be heavy enough
with cuttings.
All my love,
Your loving
Mother

Editor's note: the envelope for this letter was marked OPENED BY CENSOR
and stamped NO SERVICE – RETURN TO SENDER and returned to PGK's
mother dated 9 May 1942.

To: Capt P G Kendall
1/17th Dogra Regiment
c/o Hong Kong & Shanghai Bank
Sungei Patani
Kedah
Malaya

Arashiyama
Grantown-on-Spey
Morayshire

15th December 1941

No. 97

My darling Peter
How dreadfully the war has advanced since I last wrote to you, but
I am trying to emulate your bravery, and I trust in God for your
safety throughout this terrible time. If I hadn't that sure faith in His
goodness to those who trust himutterly, I don't know what I should
do, but as I said in my last cable to you it helps me more than I
can possibly say, so don't worry about me darling, as I am all right.
I am only getting my just share of what other mothers had had to
go through for months – some even years – and for your sake I am
remaining brave and hopeful. I have heaps of work to do here, for
which I am thankful, and my time is fully occupied with war work. I
have made many good friends so am never lonely.

I was at Mrs Grant-Smith's for tea yesterday. Her husband is
a retired Colonel, now Factor of Seafield Estates. He was most
optimistic about the outcome of the war as I also am. They are very
delightful people and most kind. Mrs Grant-Smith is in my shift
at the canteen. I think I told you I am always taken by car to the
canteen and back again, so I haven't to walk in the blackout.

We are knitting this fortnight for the Russians, and I have just
finished a pair of gumboot stockings. They are knitted in very thick
oiled wool and we have a fortnight to knit them, but I have managed
to do mine in a week, so will try to get some more wool at the depot
today and do another pair. There's not much work in them as being
such thick wool they come on very quickly.

Mrs Matteson, the woman who has the Forbes house, is expecting
her son home from Singapore any day now. He had been there for
over 4 years and was in the Air Force. He got leave about a month
before hostilities started, his former leave a few months before that
having been suddenly cancelled. She is very overjoyed of course, but

anxious about his safe passage in these times. I am going to meet him on his return and get what news he can give me of Singapore. Mr McGregor, who owns this house, has not heard from her son for a year. He is a planter out there, but was in former years an officer in the Seaforths. Tried to rejoin his regiment when war broke out but couldn't, so joined one of the regiments out there. I don't know if you ever came across him. Noel McGregor and he must be between 40 and 50 I should think. It's too bad he never writes home, as his mother is terribly worried, so you see dear there is always somebody worse off than me. I think it would have killed me if you had turned out like that, but that I have never had to worry about.

I wanted to send you £5 for Xmas dear. I wrote Nan (Editor's note: Nettie's oldest sister Agnes, PGK's aunt) *and asked her to see my banker and find out if it was your branch of the HK & S Bank which had been shifted to London. She got my letter on the Saturday and on the Sunday hostilities had started, so she found me on the Monday to say Mr Adams had said it would be most unsafe to send it, in fact he wouldn't care to do it. So it will keep for you dear. I don't suppose it would be of any use to you now at any rate. I will send it when the war is over and you can celebrate in Bombay, DV.*

Well, no more meantime darling. My thoughts and prayers are for you all the time, as are all the family's. Nan tells me she prays for you every night. Keep hopeful all the time. War always starts darkly, but it will brighten and improve as Russia and Libia (?) have done, and we are all in God's keeping, and must put our trust and faith in Him, as I know you do.
All my love
Your loving
Mother
P.S. I am sending this by the quick rate, so you will get it probably before my previous one.

Editor's note: the envelope for this letter was stamped NO SERVICE – RETURN TO SENDER and returned to PGK's mother dated 14th June 1942.

120

To: Capt P G Kendall
1/17th Dogra Regiment
c/o Hong Kong & Shanghai Bank
Sungei Patani
Kedah
Malaya

Arashiyama
Grantown-on-Spey
Morayshire

29th December 1941

No. 98

My darling Peter
This will be my last letter of this year, which I am glad to see the
end of. I hope this next one will be better for us all, and bring us
nearer to brighter days. As my Minister said on Sunday, God is in
command, and we can only find hope by trusting in Him. Certainly
it has helped me more than I can say, as I could never have found
this hope and bravery had I not had confidence in your being in His
hands. It is not like me to write like this, but the world has become
such a holocaust, and we must have faith in God, or the anxiety of
us mothers would be unbearable. I have had letters from several,
and they all think as I do. It's the only thing which can save this
world from destruction, and the people here are all turning back to
the Church. Certainly our King is a fine example, but I don't suppose
you would hear his Christmas Day broadcast.

I had a letter and two boxes of chocolates from Mrs Burns, as
Billy (Editor's note: Billy Burns, brother of John Burns, and Nettie's
boyfriend) *had sent her more than she could eat. She had phoned*
Nan to ask if any word from you, as she didn't know where John
was as she always wrote c/o Finlay's (Editor's note: James Finlay &
Co., PGK's company)*. Nan phoned me and told me so I immediately*
wrote and told her not to worry unduly as I knew from one of your
letters John was at least 80 miles from where the fighting was going
on, as you had mentioned calling on him when on your special job,
although you hadn't been able to tell me what this job was or the
name of the place John was stationed at, but had said it was 80
miles from SP and that he wouldn't be in this first awful fighting. I
had such a nice letter back from her, with the chocolates, saying my
letter had helped her so much, and made her feel ashamed of her
despondency when she read how bravely I was carrying on. I feel so

sorry for her, as she is all alone, and too old to do war work. I am thankful to have mine, as my days are fully occupied. I have four different jobs now, canteen, Red Cross collecting, and distributing cod liver oil and black currant juice to children under 2 years of age. This is given free and the mothers bring them to the distribution centre. I have also knitted 2 pairs of gumboot stockings for the Russians. We had only a fortnight to do them so it was a rush as I could only do them at intervals between my other work.

I have also made a record in Grantown with my collecting. Last month I had £3.17.6 (Editor's note: 3 pounds, 17 shillings and 6 pence in old money) and the other boxes had mostly 15/– to 30/– (Editor's note: 15 shillings to 30 shillings, old money). So the bank manager congratulated me, and said I must be a most conscientious collector. This month has been for Russia and I have collected over £6. I don't know if I gave you all this news in my last letter, as I have so many letters, and have had so many to answer at this time I can't remember what I told you. I sent it by Clipper which cost 5/– (Editor's note: 5 shillings old money) but worth it, as it goes so much quicker, and I wanted you to get it soon to let you know I am all right. I am in such excellent health with my long stay in this lovely air, and my nerves now completely cured. Had this happened 18 months ago, I'd probably have been a nervous wreck, or had a beakdown.

Nan has phoned and asked me if I'd not like to go home for New Year, also Burns (Editor's note: PGK's only uncle, Nettie's youngest, only, brother) wrote saying they'd be delighted to have me, but I'm not going. I'm much happier here with my various jobs and I have so many good friends, and am invited out a lot. I was at an Xmas party in the church last night for the soldiers and evacuees. I was helping with the tea and arranging games, etc. It was a great success. All the troops in good form and all stone cold sober. Of course, Grantown is practically dry and only one drink allowed in the hotels, and none to be bought which is a good thing! So there will be very little first footing with bottles in Glasgow this year. Nan says even she can't get any, as it is all being sent to America to help pay for armaments. So I expect people will just go to bed at a reasonable hour, as Nan says she is doing, and thankful she will be able to!

I am hoping this will reach you, dear, as no use sending to Sungei

*Patani, but have put yur regiment in the hope it will find you. I
hope you got my three cables. I got yours and was thankful to get
them, but don't expect any from you now for some time. You have
certainly got your chance of fighting for your country darling, as you
were longing to do, and I, and all the family including your Father*
(Editor's note: PGK's mother and father – Percy – were separated when
he was two years old, and subsequently divorced) *are very proud of you.
I had a letter from him saying he was very worried about you and
asking me to send him any news I get from you. Theo has been home
on embarkation leave and Mrs Grant is in a terrible state, but we all
have to go through it, and we must keep brave. All the family – even
Norman* (Editor's note: Norman Munro, Nettie's brother-in-law, married
to her youngest sister, PGK's Aunt Marjorie) *are astonished at what
they call my bravery, but it is only my great faith which keeps me up.
All my love darling, and God watch over you.
Your loving
Mother*

Editor's note: the envelope for this letter bore an Air Mail sticker with the
handwritten words *Via North Atlantic and Trans Pacific Air Service,* also
stamped POST EARLY FOR CHRISTMAS. It was returned to PGK's mother
stamped NO SERVICE – RETURN TO SENDER.

To: Capt P G Kendall
1/17th Dogra Regiment
C/o Hong Kong & Shanghai Bank
Sungei Patani
Kedah
Malaya

Arashiyama
Grantown-on-Spey
Morayshire

8th January 1941

My darling Peter,
I posted a long letter to you a few days ago, and the stupid people
at the Post Office here told me it could not go airmail now as that
was stopped, so had to send by boat which will take a very long time.
Nan was on the phone and I asked her to find out if that was the
case. She enquired in Glasgow and I find out it is not true.

I am so angry at the PO here for misleading, as they said they
were positive. However, am writing again and will give them a bit
of my mind when I go to post it. I also wrote you by "Clipper" after
the Japs attacked, as it goes very much quicker that way, by paying
5/– (Editor's note: five shilling in old money) *but worth it for that letter*
as I wanted you to know I m all right, and my faith in God taking
care of you is a tremendous help to me.

The PO people told me then that the 5/- Clipper service to
Malaya was stopped, but I sent the letter to Nan and she found it
was still on so sent it off for me from there. I hope you got it before
hostilities reached your part, but I'm afraid dear, you were very near
the start of operations, and I know now you will be in the very thick
of it, but I can only trust and pray for you, as we are all doing.

Nan phoned to ask if I was not going home for Xmas, but I
didn't go as nothing to do there and too much time to think. Here I
am kept very busy with Canteen, Red Cross collecting, distributing
cod liver oil to children, which the Government gives free, knitting
for troops, etc, so my day is fully occupied.

I was on the Canteen Hogmanay evening, but the troops were
very quiet and well behaved. They played the piano and sang as
usual. I wanted to go to the midnight service in the chuch, which
is just five minutes walk from here, so Miss McDonald and I went
– a gorgeous night of glistening frost and full moon – and had a
very impressive service. Several of the soldiers who had been in the
Canteen were there.

New Year's Day we went to the morning service in the English Church. We had a very nice Xmas dinner of turkey, plum pudding and all the bits, and a nice glass of clean cold water to wash it down! I usually have Orange Crush or Rose's Lime Juice Cordial on my table, but was so busy at that time had forgotten to replenish.

Theo (Grant) has been home on embarkation leave, and Marjorie (Editor's note: Marjorie Munro, Nettie's youngest sister, PGK's auntie) *tells me Mrs Grant is in a terrible state as not being strong, she thought he would be kept in this country. I am terribly sorry for her, but we mothers have all to go through this awful ordeal.*

I am thankful I came here as my health is now perfect, and my old troubles, nerves, completely cured, so am much more able to stand the strain of anxiety than I would have been had it happened 18 months ago. It is all very terrible darling, and I know you must be going through a horrible experience but keep up your heart dear, and have faith in God as I have. It's the only staying power in this awful crisis, and the only thing that can bring us through. Our King sets us a fine example.

Things have started badly for us in many instances, and there have been many, what one might call miracles, such as Dunkirk, the Battle of Britain, and even Libya and Russia. All fought against tremendous odds, and they all started badly for us, but all are on the way to victory and Malaya will do the same.

Meantime you, and those with you, have to fight against overwhelming odds, which must require tremendous courage and endurance, which I know you have. Now that Wavell is in command the tide will turn I am sure and everybody here with sons or husbands in Malaya is praying for that day.

Your father has written me several times for news of you. He is very worried about you, and very sympathetic regarding what he knows I must be going through.

I think I am more or less repeating my letter of a few days ago, but this will reach you sooner. I have of course no address, but am outing your Regiment on the envelope, and asking to forward, hoping it will go to wherever your bank has been moved to, and so reach you.

I have just received your letter dated 15th Octr. I loved getting it and hearing all your interesting news, but I can't help wishing it were all happening now, instead of what is happening. Burns (Editor's note: Nettie's, only, younger, brother, PGK's uncle) *also had a letter from you, which he sent on for me to read. The family all sent you cables at Xmas which I hope you got.*

Well darling, no more news. Remember I am always thinking of you, and praying for your safety. As our Minister said on Sunday the greed of the world has brought on this war, but God is in control, and if we believe that, we can have no doubts. I know it has helped me more than I could ever have thought possible.
All my love darling,
Your loving
Mother

Editor's note: the envelope for this letter bore an Air Mail sticker and was stamped IT IS REGRETTED THAT THIS LETTER COULD NOT BE DELIVERED AT THE ADDRESS STATED and was returned to PGK's mother.

Printed in the United Kingdom
by Lightning Source UK Ltd.
125077UK00001B/9/A